ALL THAT I AM: NOW THAT I KNOW

✓ 17 LIFE LESSONS *for Women Entrepreneurs on Dreaming Big, Failing Big, and dusting off your ass to DO IT all over again!*

TERESA SPANGLER

ISBN: 9781799035763

DEDICATION:

To my beautiful daughter who inspires me to live my truth, love life, and continue to grow and travel the world; and to my incredible, intelligent, idea-generating machine of a husband—our world's rock on change for a better world!

My Promise & Commitment

Authenticity has become such a buzzword of late overused and under-delivered in many cases. I commit to being authentic. You will immediately know I stay true to this.

It's not about me, but my experiences. These are the lessons I share. You get to your truth, your mission, and shine big—hopefully much faster and a little easier.

Readers of this book care! You care about positive change in the world. You care about equality. You care about giving and mentoring and helping others achieve their dreams on your path to achieving your dreams.

I hope the lessons I've learned provide you with nuggets of insights and inspiration as we build a powerful community.

I promise to respond to emails and answer burning questions to help you on your journey. Please be patient—answering emails might take a bit of response time.

Special Thanks!

I am not sure this book would have been born without my good friend Shawn Ramsey. Thank you for all your encouragement, feedback and for the magic crystals and wonderful inspiration. Also thank you Brian Ference for your support and feedback.

TABLE OF CONTENTS

CHAPTER 1.

INTRODUCTION

My name is Teresa Spangler. I'm what you would call a challenge junkie. Others have challenged me all my life. "Ain't no woman made it yet in this business and you won't either!" they said to me. I took that challenge and beat out 240 men to become the number one saleswoman in that company. In the early nineties, venture capitalists (VCs) simply did not fund women in technology. I accepted that challenge and went on to get funding. In another move, I joined a start-up that grew from $23 million in revenue to $400 million in less than five years. I am currently a member of the Forbes Technology Council.

Before the #Metoo movement, I was overcoming groping by company founders of a start-up I was leading and went on to codevelop one of the first Linux software–driven web-serving appliances. Since then I've held executive positions at Red Hat Software and was responsible for leading revenue growth pre- and post-IPO. In addition, I have founded and led several entrepreneurial organizations through growth milestones, including venture capital funding, IPOs, innovation creation, and development of strategies leveraging technology.

I grew from rags to riches, making millions and then watching it all disappear. When I turned fifty years old, I realized that my life seemed like a failure, because I had not dared to dream big enough. What few dreams I had left, had been little more than scrawled down wishes with no real detail or plan on how to accomplish it. Then, I re-invented myself and made my lifelong dream happen by creating a business and nonprofit organization that created showcase opportunities for more than two hundred original artists and musicians. We produced shows over seven years, capturing the attention of New York dance communities and globally known musicians.

I have pulled from my successes and failures to provide powerful strategies and exercises that may guide you through your personal journey on the road to achieving big dreams, whether that be in love, life, in the business world, creating wealth, or merely gaining that inner peace we are all searching for.

CHAPTER 2.

HIKE TILL YOUR MIND
GOES EMPTY

Quiet engulfs me. Roosters clock in on time. The breezy overcast climate calls for my Patagonia warm pullover. The weight on my back is heavier than I ever anticipated, and everything is starting on an uphill climb. Is this a metaphor for life? Am I nuts? I have no emotions, no anxiety, no worries, no thoughts of forced mindfulness. This is just the beginning of a long journey hiking from little town to little town.

Our final destination is Santiago de Compostela, Spain. My means of transportation are my two feet trekking more than eighteen to twenty miles a day. Starting my journey, I feel strangely at peace. I don't even know why. After all I've been through in my life, the journey by foot up mountains and down mountains somehow feel oddly like life's journey itself. I expected my monkey mind would take over while walking from small Spanish town to small Spanish town. But there's not a thought bubble popping. Pilgrims, we are all pilgrims, on the search for a sense of inner peace.

I was hiking with my husband of thirty-two years over sixteen to twenty miles daily. We hiked some of the most beautiful peaks and valleys I've ever seen through the rural parts of northern Spain. From the very start, I am in awe of the landscape, the serenity, the mooing cows, whinnying horses, barking dogs, goats bahing—a quiet, peaceful silence, with the exception of nature's orchestra. Narrow path with markers of blue tiles painted with the emblem of a seashell points the way for pilgrims on 780 kilometers—nearly 500 miles—on the Camino de Santiago. There are six paths of varying distances to the cherished end, Santiago de Compostela. We chose the original Spanish route. This path allowed us to hike the time we had off yet still earn our Certificate of completion known as the Compostela. Our final destination would be the Saint James Cathedral. Jesus's apostle James is said to be buried in this cathedral.

The long original journey of the Camino de Santiago path dates back to the early ninth century—814, to be exact. This is when the tomb of Saint James the Great, an evangelical apostle from the Iberian Peninsula, was discovered. The early discovery of Santiago de Compostela, which in the present day can take up to forty-five days to hike, is the journey point not just for the entire European continent but also for more than 300,000 pilgrims. Over 280,000 hikers receive Compostela certificates of completion yearly. To receive a certificate, a hiker must hike a minimum of one hundred kilometers or cycle the last two hundred kilometers.

On the Camino journey, we rarely saw any cars but often saw herds of cows passing at any given moment. Stone walls protect the modest, ancient stone homes lined with the colors of summer: hydrangeas, roses of every color, fuchsia, bright yellow, and blue-and-pink varietal flowers. The colorful plant and animal life represent a rich history of pilgrims who have walked these trails for generations. I feel these colors represent the richness in life. Floral covered walls encircle communities keeping the cows, goats, and chickens on their own turfs welcoming strangers as we walk the historical trail running through the backyards of rural farmers of Spain, France, Italy, and Portugal.

Hiking feels wonderfully lazy though interestingly strenuous. Each day seems to go faster than imagined. Sun-filled evenings have a Spanish-linger to them, leisurely slow. Shoes are the first thing to come off! After the shoes, I peel off the salt-crusted dry-fit hiking clothes from my sweaty back, then immediately wash them and then me. After dressing in my second of the only two pairs of pants in my backpack, I enjoy an excellent glass of table rioja costing less than two dollars per glass or ten dollars per bottle, rub my feet slowly, and then hang the wash to dry on a 1950s clothesline.

Part of me would love to just keep hiking until the second glass of Spanish rioja overtook my body, rendering me useless. Others joined at our table for some cherished storytelling. Pilgrims from all over the world traveling the same route. Slowly my thoughts and my emotions settle into the feeling of great gratitude. Every step is a step forward. Every step forward is one step closer to the goal of reaching Santiago.

It's all metaphorical for life as every step is a step on our journey of life. My toenails eventually turn black and blue, my feet ache in pain the more miles I walk. My mind gets lost on what day it is. When I am reaching for big dreams on an entrepreneurial pilgrimage of sorts, my journey feels similar. Without maps, the right shoes, great planning, gathering the most important resources one needs all along the path, coupled with a real passion for the long trek ahead, you may never reach the ultimate destination or realize our personal or entrepreneur's quest. At least, in this case, the destination was clear. The path was already laid out for me. That is certainly not the case with most entrepreneurs. My journey has certainly taken a number of unexpected turns.

In the chapters ahead, I will share stories of my own experiences. Many of these stories I revisited in my journal during my pilgrimage realizing my experiences, mistakes, successes, and failures may help others. Each chapter will have some tips and strategies I hope will help you on your own personal journey, your pilgrimage through life, and on your personal path to achieving big dreams.

Planning a journey is critical to making the experience the best it can be.

CHAPTER 3.

JOURNEYING AND JOURNALING

Journeying and journaling—these two exercises go hand in hand. Frequent journaling, releasing any thoughts that come to mind on paper, will help to generate new ideas from the depths of our souls if we stick with writing every morning. Writing regularly may surface deep passions, new desires, and foster a renewed creativity within us. Journeying is an opportunity to broaden our experiences and feed us creative fuel for our journal exercises. Your journeys do not need to be in a foreign country. Your experiences could be broadened by doing new things you've never done or have not done in a long time like going to a museum or watching a documentary on a topic that interests you. The exercises in this book all involve journaling and some journeying. Enjoy the process!

We'll start here with a thoughtful exercise of considerations. As we move on, you'll be encouraged to engage deeply in the exercises that follow. The exercise below gives us a foundation for the journey of entrepreneurship.

Stop for a few minutes to contemplate the following eleven points. Savor these, then come back to review them as you go through the other exercises:

EXERCISE 1: HIKING THE CAMINO DE SANTIAGO OF ENTREPRENEURIAL SUCCESS

You may hike in your own backyard, or hike the Camino, or just mentally visualize your own dreamy, quiet journey! Reflect on these eleven keys to mapping a successful journey, be it a hike or a dream or starting a new business.

Start Here:

1. Mapping the way before you start. Research, research, and more research is so important.

2. Define a clear endpoint. How will you know you've succeeded?

3. Multiple routes all lead to the same endpoint. Different teams can take each route and still end up with the same results.

4. You can always go further and endure more if you have a mission.

5. Enjoy the path, the journey.

6. Technology is your friend in times of need; otherwise put it all down.

7. Rest is the most important thing on long journeys.

8. Meeting people from all walks of life feeds your soul and your mind.

9. The sun does not always shine—be prepared.

10. If you meet a cow, milk it; if you see a bear, stop and play dead; if you hear a tractor, it's probably fifty years old or older and still kicking.

Stop at every bar—they are all different and unique. Each will stamp your Camino passport with a new experience. Log in to your life: no password required. Find the joy everywhere you can on any journey you make!

CHAPTER 4.

I DID NOT DREAM BIG ENOUGH

The heart of the matter is this: I did not dream big enough at the start of my professional life. I am proud of what I've accomplished—cool work, financial successes, and beautiful family. But at the heart of the matter, I realized that as I was entering my late forties and early fifties, I clearly did not dream big enough. I did not dream about specific details. I did not write down enough of the imagery. I rarely shared my intentions with close friends who could have helped me along. I'm not sure I even understood what setting intentions meant in those years.

What would I share with my younger self? Dream bigger! That I should expose myself to more journeys, alone and with others! In order to dream bigger, I also need to experience bigger—not just exploring places but experiences with diverse groups of people, including creative people, analytical people, musicians, and artists. I consider myself incredibly fortunate to have had a hungry appetite to seek out new, always teetering on the edge trends. I never had a fear of approaching anyone. I recognize now I often held myself back.

Looking back, I now know I created an invisible ceiling over my head, self-imposing unreal limitations in my younger years. I felt unstoppable. But what I know now is that I held myself back. Ways we hold ourselves back are often subliminal. Let me share a few of these ways here:

HOW MIGHT YOU BE HOLDING YOURSELF BACK?

Here is an example of how imposter syndrome can sabotage your path forward. I had finally convinced a VC, who happened to suggest I design a product out of what we called the "wall of technology"—technology ideas outlined on a whiteboard-thus our wall—to fund the development team and me. The first product I designed was one of the first web and email-server appliances to ever run on Linux. Our start-up was founded at nearly the same time Red Hat Software was also becoming popular, but more on this later.

The VC had confidence I could figure out how to make a go of this very early stage start-up. He had confidence I could lead the technology founder forward and that I could also get the company to revenue growth. I knew this from many conversations we'd had together. This was the early nineties, when VCs did not fund women, especially women in tech. I felt incredibly fortunate. And you must also know, even though he encouraged me, believed in me, I still had to nearly choke him to get him to write a check!

Before he put pen to paper, he asked me one killer question: "Who will lead the company?" My answer, the *killer answer*, "I don't know! We will have to find a CEO." Deep down I knew he was asking me to step up, yet I felt imposter syndrome take over every mental brain cell and body part I had. I did not just step back, I stepped down. I was immediately disappointed in myself. It was a fleeting moment of feeling it was the biggest mistake of my life. Did the world change immediately at that moment? No, the relationship stayed the same, the funds were provided. I had a wonderful experience, but I always look back at that moment and wonder what if I'd said me! I can lead this company.

What could you do to shield your brain from suffering from imposter syndrome? Exercising our minds to be strong when your gut is churning and burning with anxiety and you think you may throw up? What are these feelings that potentially sabotage your own success?

22

Throughout the book, I will share some exercises I have created over the years to help me build mental confidence and a more trusting gut instinct! One of the most important components of these exercises is writing. You've heard it over and over again. There is a reason!

Writing provides clarity if you write enough. I'll share a lot about this later in the book, but for now, know there is no exercise without these five components:

1. **Writing**

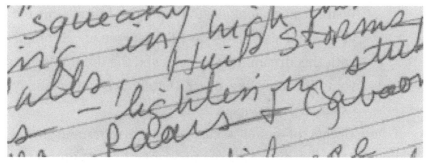

2. **Reflecting**
3. **Meditation**: Slowing down your mind however you want to achieve this: yoga, hiking, sitting by the fire, etc.
4. **Dreaming**
5. **Repeat** as often as you want but no less than every six months. This provides a check-in with yourself.

Let's get started with the first very important exercise: *dreaming!*

DREAMING BIG EXERCISE 2: GROWING YOUR DREAM BANK

- Have you identified your big dreams? What are three dreams you have right now? Write these down. What were three dreams you had at age seventeen or eighteen? Write these down.
- Would you know how to create a bigger dream? Pick one of the above dreams and expand on the dream. Where are you? Who benefits from your dream?
  - o Write a page looking out into the future—an old but very good exercise—on all that you've accomplished with this dream. You've achieved the dream! What does your life look like now? Details are important. Write using all your senses.
- If you dream of being a successful entrepreneur have you defined clearly what that picture looks like? Where are you? What city? Where is your home? What is it like? Where is your office? What is in your office? Who are you working with? How does it all feel to you? Be as specific as possible. Is your office painted yellow with a big white leather couch?

Visualization writing is such a strong exercise. This is one to write and forget for a while. Write and then put your writings in a safe place. You may pull them out from time to time to remind yourself of these dreams.

Spend time to really visualize your dream. Write them down.

Add clear details; then consider how they might be uplifted. For example, if you want to have the most successful cupcake company in your town, how might you grow your dream? If you want to grow it maybe you just want to make that one store the most spectacular store in the town. Whatever your dreams are today, spend the time to consider more details, adding more clarity, considering if they are "big fucking hairy, audacious dreams" you are passionate about pursuing.

1. Ask yourself what it is you really want in life? Do you have a dream you are holding yourself back from realizing this dream in some way? What might be holding you back?

2. List ten reasons you feel you are holding back; then list ten people or actions you could take to help you move forward.

3. Write down the top three things that could happen if you don't accomplish this big thing in the timeframe you want to achieve?

4. Ask yourself: Is the time frame realistic? Am I giving myself time?

5. What in my power do I need to do to succeed at this big thing?

    a. Can I take a course that will help?

    b. Who could I ask for help?

c. Seek out peers and tell them your intentions. By telling your intentions to others you become more accountable to yourself: to hold your own feet to the fire. Check-in with those you shared your intentions with from time to time.

d. Ask yourself, am I stopping myself? Why? White down the whys!

Big Dreams Are Made of Sugar and Spice and Everything Nice! RIGHT?

There is a big, wonderful world out there. Broadening one's worldly perspectives is important to dreaming big. That does not mean you have to travel the world at all or all the time. Reading, exploring videos, talking and networking can help with the broadening of perspectives.

Dreams, not one dream, are important. One dream is not enough. Dreams move, change, and evolve over time. How about the journey? Who writes down the journey one can imagine taking on the way to a dream or to dreams? I don't even remember writing my journey down clearly until I was in my forties. I wrote down my goals, I wrote out dream concepts, but I did not visualize the details. What I got from the universe were incomplete dreams. Let me explain. My dream for my idea, The Creativity House, has been a lifelong dream. I describe it as a dreamy landscape, large Italian stone villa that houses no more than twelve to twenty people, a retreat, resort, and getaway for musicians

and creative people looking to be inspired and to inspire. They may be writing their first or fifth book. They may be composing the next big jazz composition, or scripting the next Broadway play or TV comedy series. All the musical equipment, recording and sound room, writer's library and creative nooks and crannies a creative person could ever dream of would be there for them to freely explore. We would locate my dream in the mountains or against the backdrop of ocean views.

This dream was written at the age of sixteen, rewritten in more detail at the age of twenty-two, and then again at thirty-five. I actually founded Creative Leadership Adventures and at the same time a not for profit Night of Dreams arts organization at the age of forty-four, moving my plans forward with the Creativity House Resort. Shortly after I started my business and the creative nonprofit, someone I used to work with, who only knew I had a passion for the arts and music, invited me to my dream! I was blown away as I visited the building site, saw the plans and listened to his dream. With tears in his eyes, the instant he started sharing blueprints of his dream of creating a retreat for musicians, I realized my *big* mistake. I am standing in my dream! I was not specific about who owned the dream! Who would benefit, myself included? How would it inspire me as we served others? In other words, I left myself out of my dream!

Writing and dreaming is a fun exercise. When clarity, vision, and passion all collide into a dream, it can be a powerful and sometimes scary thing. As the saying goes, be careful what you ask for. In my writing of my own dreams, I have learned that I must write about what the dream means to me. I need to write about my role in the dream. Do I own the dream? Is it my business, or am I participating in the dream? In the case above, I left out important details about my Creativity House Dream. I only wrote about the house's features and benefits. I did not write about my role in the house! What would it mean to me to create this house? How long would I own the house, and how many people could I and my creativity resort of sorts impact?

Journey

This grand journey in life and the routes to the realization of dreams may falter. Wrong turns, roadblocks, cliffs may prevent you from reaching a final destination. Was I prepared for the failures of not realizing particular dreams as a young girl? Nope, not in the least. Not reaching a goal, however, was never particularly debilitating. Therein lies the issue! I simply did not *dream big enough*.

What I know now is the bigger you dream, the more detail you visualize and write about your dream, the more passionate you become about that dream. Passion has the power of turning dreams into action. Dreaming bigger has the power to achieve shorter-term milestones that prepare you for your bigger dream. For example, say you want to be an astronaut and one day land on Mars. Do you fail if you land on the Moon first? No, the moon landing is a stepping-stone for the next big step in your dream: Mars. But wait, how would I have known what a big dream was? What are big dreams? Why do we need to dream big?

Dreams, I believe, are mastered from what we know at the time we know it. Influences may be things like economic conditions, where you live, news coverage you have access to, upbringing, and education. Outside influences or influencers shape our desires, our goals and ultimately our dreams. It could be Bono influencing us to be the next U2, or it could be going to college in America to find a better life if you live in Africa or Southeast Asian, where women are not treated—or are terribly mistreated, as the case may be—as equals.

We dream what we know. I knew I wanted to go to college, make a lot of money, live in Denver someday, ski the rest of my life, travel, and be the female version of Bruce Springsteen! Were these dreams or goals? The lessons begin with this question as a foundation. My journey travels you through successes and epic failures. By the way, I did move to Denver for a very large opportunity of a lifetime! A dream of mine had always been to live in Denver. I never wrote specifically visualizing this dream, I wanted to live in Denver, *Colorado*! I ended up in Denver, North Carolina. Be specific in documenting your dreams!

Focus on Learning and Growth

I had, and continue to have, ferocious appetite for learning new things. But my greatest fear kept me from being a multi-degreed individual. My two greatest fears in life are: forgetting the words to songs when I am performing and failing tests—any test including those pesky little surveys you can't help taking on Facebook that tell you what movie star you are most like or the country you should live in. The truth is, I ball up in my gut tightly! I feel as though I'm going to throw up when facing a quiz or a test.

It was like finding gold when I discovered the power of massively open online courses (MOOCs). I have become a MOOC junky. Coursera, Edx, Udemy—I love them all. The best part, I can take and retake their quizzes over and over again if the material is particularly difficult. What I have recently learned about learning from one of my favorite courses on learning from Coursea is retaking quizzes and self-pacing is actually one of the best ways to retain the material. I love learning new things. Learning for me is about personal growth. Personal growth feeds a certain energy in me that helps keep the drive, enthusiasm, energy, excitement, and creativity alive in everything I do.

Growth is a big factor for dreamers. There are many possible pitfalls on the journey to achieving our greatest desires and goals. Keeping the mind fresh is a self-preservation action. If one door slams in my face, there is a feeling of continued growth by learning new things and charting a new map on the path forward.

Take it from a learning junkie: read and take courses to keep your mind active, as the path to dreams is one of always learning.

A few thoughts from the *Learning Junkie's Corner—Feeding the Growth Mind-Set*:

Read, read, and read some more. Don't just listen to audiobooks. Read books, magazines, white papers, and research, reports. Read everything you can get your hands on about topics that interest you. Keep reading until you have exhausted your interest levels, then switch topics.

Explore other mediums covering your interests: YouTube is a gold mine. Too few people explore the depths of what YouTube has to offer. For example, explore the YouTube Creator Academy channel to learn how to create your own YouTube channel. Or watch Google Talks on YouTube where they feature guest speakers to inspire Google employees. They record these to share with the world. Authors, comedians, musicians, and experts from around the globe share stories and insights.

EXERCISE 3: TAKE THREE CREATIVE ONLINE COURSES

1. But don't stop at YouTube. Find courses that interest you on Coursea or Edx. You can audit most for free or achieve certifications at a low cost. Or, if you are inclined, you could gain another degree.

   Here is a list of the Best MOOC Platforms of 2018 according to Reviews.com:

Rank	Site Name	Total
#1	Coursera	9.5
#2	edX	6.6
#3	Udacity	6.3
#4	FutureLearn	5.6
#5	iversity.org	2.7
#6	Cognitive Class	1.2

2. Put a lesson you have learned from the class or video into action! One of my favorite learning sites for inspiration is MASTERCLASS.com. All are wonderful. The cooking lessons

from the likes of great chefs like Chef Gordon Ramsay inspires me and sparks my creative side!

    a. Make one of the meals from a cooking class you watched online. Or take a cooking course.

    b. Sign up for one of the many comedy classes. Now play a bit and work on your own comedy script? Just have fun with this exercise.

3. Allow yourself to mess up and have fun with the process! This is not an effort of achieving perfection but an activity that opens up new parts of you.

Falling in and out of Passions: Divers versus Skimmers

Are you a skimmer or a diver? Skimmers acquire new passions that are sometimes short-lived. An example might be, scuba diving. You want to learn to dive. You take one course, get certified. Then decide to move on to paragliding. After one trip you can decide to pick up the guitar, take one lesson and then on to drums and so on. You never dive deep into mastery. Divers are individuals who plunge deeply into a subject or a hobby. They are nearly, if not positively, obsessed with their areas of interest, reaching mastery levels. But not just mastering this new hobby. Divers buy every gadget and read every book on the topic. They search for the experts to talk it up. Some divers cannot move past over this new hobby until they feel they are all-knowing.

I loved to skim and know a lot of things about a lot of different things. Reading Malcolm Gladwell's book *Outliers: The Story of Success*, he talks about how it takes ten thousand hours to achieve mastery— an-eye-opening book for me. I spent time exploring my ten thousand hours in two ways:

1. I spent a great deal of time documenting where I had ten thousand hours of knowledge and experience.
2. I also spent time understanding where I had only skimmed the surface. This prompted me to dive deeper into areas in which I wanted to be an expert.

Placing my attention on when to dive versus skim was an important part of my evolution. I found myself adding a third level I call, "skiving" not quite diving deeply but not skimming over the surface either. Why and when is "skiving" relevant?

Hobbies are fun activities for everyone! I choose hobbies I want to get better and better at over time. I always want music in my life. Over my lifetime, I will continue lessons, better my musical abilities, and practice whenever possible. Learning never feels like a burden or a job to me. Music is not about making money. I am investing in myself! Here are my thoughts on when to use skimming versus diving versus skiving.

The Hobbyist

I proposed the blended option skiving, where you become someone who has a deep understanding of topics. You are active in new hobbies, but not so obsessed that your focus is only on that one thing. Skiving may allow you to hold on to a passion with continued interest and personal growth for a lifetime.

The Entrepreneur

Taking one step back here, as an entrepreneur, I propose that divers are completely obsessed and passionate that their business ideas will navigate their way to winning! I found this to be true in my own life too. Relentless diving is simply a necessity! However, you can hire great divers to help you not be consumed. More on this later.

The Interested Bystander

Show me the money was an early driver, but not with compromising of my happiness and believing in what I did or who I worked for.

My life was linear growing up. I went to school to go to college, I went to college to get a good job when I got out of college. I'd get a good job that would pay me so I could save money to retire. At the time I didn't even know what that meant, and I went to church to gain faith in the world. I went to music lessons to play for church and to have something in my life that would be with me all my life. I played tennis on the tennis team because, well, I just loved the fact that I was good and could win. And, I grew up competitive because I had five brothers and, well, we were competitive!

I went to school, I went to college, I graduated, and I got a job—any job, because that is what you did. I remained competitive because that is was what I was, and I learned over time. I never thought of being a woman in the workplace because my brothers never treated me any differently than they treated each other. We competed, we laughed, and we worked together in my father's businesses. We were all encouraged to believe we could do anything if we put our minds to it.

And I stop here to share the buts in my life. But you must make a living. But you need more education to do that job and make a good living. Anytime I said I wanted to be a musician, there was always a but from the mouths of my elders. But you must get a job and make a living. "You can be a musician, but you must get a job and make money to live on."

Buts are detrimental to dreams if we allow them to be. *But* is a safety word. But stop, drop, and roll! But think about it. But why would you do that? But I have a better idea, but no! The word *but* protects us from the risk of failure, risk of not realizing a dream and from risking hurt or loss. But's are important and should be heard. That does not mean a but should stop us from pursuing our passions. I know now, I could have blended both. I could have pursued musical endeavors while also working and making a living for myself. I know now, how I could have done both but at the time it felt nearly impossible to have a career to make a living and also having music in my life.

I wish I knew then what I know now about the buts of my life. I heard these words, internalized the words that followed the but, and in some cases *stopped in my tracks* to pivot to safety.

Don't ever stop at the but!

Fun: When the Fun Is Depleted

Every passion potentially becomes depleted in us if we do not put rubber bumpers around our psyches'. What do I mean by this? Let's look at the life of an artist turned entrepreneur. The world of TWS— me, Teresa Williams Spangler—Productions is one filled with ready, cameras, and action! For more than twenty-five years this passionate producer has had eyes behind the camera. The set in front of the camera is designed to elicit a particular emotion for the viewer. Every photograph emotes some feeling—sadness, heartwarming love, anger, etc. The camera allows her to fill her soul with creative expression. However, being paid to create for someone else sometimes turns into a chore. It becomes the business of photography rather than a passionate endeavor. How is one to guard themselves against passions gone awry?

For me, I love working with companies, helping individuals grow, and tackling the toughest challenges possible. I'm often referred to as a challenge junkie who loves new technologies and creative ways to solve these complex problems. But when the person or company on the other side of the table becomes arrogant and disrespectful—not just to me but others around the conference-room table—I turn off. My driver seat airbag pops open, I get up, and kindly walk away from such nonconstructive behavior. This has not been the case for all of my life in every situation. I find myself even today challenged with getting up and walking away.

In the vein of transparency, people sometimes hide behind a veil. The more they know about an individual, the more power it feeds to their own psyches. The lesson here is to stop, drop, and roll when you start to feel your stomach squeeze up into your chest to the point you feel your chest is going to explode into a full-blown heart attack.

I've experienced toxic environments around the country where every day one to three people were carted off to the emergency room or sent home for anxiety attacks. People—life is short! Let's take control of our own lives and choose how we are treated. If you feel stuck in a place you cannot get out of, your own passions depleted, and your driver-seat airbag deflated, what can you do?

CHAPTER 5.

STRATEGIES TO REFUEL YOUR PERSONAL PASSIONS

The first step in refueling is identifying what is truly depleting you. Victim stances, by the way, do not work here. We are always in control of how we feel but it takes work to learn this control. We may not always be in control of how we are treated in a particular moment, however.

Know Who You Are

Knowing *you are what you think* is a big part of regaining oneself, collecting composure, and replacing any negative emotions with self-assurance. One of my personal strategies is waking up every morning to a journal, writing positive affirmations to start my day off on the right foot. Meditation and mindfulness also calm me and set my mental pace for the day. Keeping this level of internal calm allows me to seek more of the passionate things I love doing, like working with people I love working with and—more than anything—identifying unhealthy feelings that come from someone or something that just does not feel right. In other words, this calming of my mind, body, and spirit allows stronger intuitive awareness on negative things that may crop up in my life. I have learned over time whether to confront the issues on my terms or walk away if there's no way to turn around the situation.

Give Your Voice A Workout

A strong voice is not always a loud voice. Conversely, a loud voice is not necessarily a strong voice. Strong voices are impact voices. Impact voices are voices that influence others. Leaders that understand how to motivate and inspire others to act leverage a language, inflection of their voices and timing on how they deliver information. They read body language and understand when to deliver a specific message for the best impact possible.

I find that some people confuse strong voices with loud voices. They are not the same. The strategy here is to practice the habits of "stronger voicing." Strong voicings include greater inflection and variation of range to help make key points, emphasis on important takeaways, softening for engaging empathy, confidence, flexibility, and so on. This is how strong voices learn to have greater impacts.

EXERCISE 4: CAPTURE THE VOICES:

ANGER, HAPPINESS, SADNESS

1. Listen to ten different videos on Youtube or watch a favorite movie. Close your eyes and listen to the voices.

2. What do you feel when you hear each actor or actress speak?

3. How does your body react?

4. What feelings did you experience with each voice you heard? If it was an angry voice how did you react? How did your body respond? What thoughts were streaming through your mind? Write these thoughts down in your journal!

5. Write two pages of the feelings you had while listening to these different voices.

What makes you feel terrific like, "I'd follow him or her anywhere"? What makes you want to run away and never look back!

CHAPTER 6.

FEED YOUR SOUL AND YOUR MICROBES

People - Connected with Purpose

That brings us to people connected with purpose. What else is there in the world but to have a purpose? Whatever your purpose in life is, there are people with common interests and similar purposes as well. Even if your current purpose is to *find* your new or renewed purpose, there are also others searching and people to connect with to help you on this path. The world is full of books, podcasts, blogs, and articles on living a life with purpose. There are meetups, mastermind groups, and next-door neighbors who sincerely want to help. Helping may be their purpose.

Our job on this earth is to connect. My personal journey has been one to connect to others and to help connect people together, to give where I can, to help who I can, and to positively impact the world as best I can. It feeds my soul! It's one of my purposes on earth but what I know now that I wish I'd known earlier is it takes more than just me. I need cheerleaders, supporters, friends, believers, boosters, and people to share my intentions with and to have them push back, offer feedback, provide positive support, and just simply be there, even if we sit in solitude.

Loneliness Is Gripping the World

There is an opportunity here for all of us to create a community or multiple communities around our passions. Or maybe your passion is bringing people together and you create communities for others. Whatever the reason, without people, we have no real purpose on earth. Even Elon Musk, founder of Tesla and SpaceX, knows he needs people around him; otherwise why offer trips to Mars when he can afford to go by himself!

There is a new kind of loneliness, however. We have little experience with but have a growing discord—our connected friends and people we socially follow. This follower mentality is depressing us as a society. We read about their great lives, watch people intimately on their travels, see what they are eating, see them in their hospital gowns and on Instagram, dressed for success or heading to the latest cool festival! It's crazy what we are sharing with the world on social media platforms. At times we really care; other times we could care less but act as though we do for fear of missing out (FOMO). Our connections may be friends, but our friends may not be all these connections.

*Health.Harvard.com reports the following: Loneliness can be contagious, just like a cold. According to a recent study, "**Alone in a Crowd: The Structure and Spread of Loneliness in a Large Social Network,**" lonely people tend to share their loneliness with others. Over time, a group of lonely, disconnected people move to the fringes of social networks. The problem is compounded because lonely people, those on the periphery, tend to lose the few contacts they have.*

The work for us to do is to get real and form bonds with real people and the community face-to-face. As an entrepreneur, it can get quite lonely. Friendships feel like they take as much work as growing your venture. Friends are important and worth the trouble. You don't need hundreds. You just need a few good close friends! In my thirties, I was feeling very alone. I'd moved to a new city, and it felt like no other working professional women lived in my area. I reached out to someone I realized lived in the area. She was one of the smartest women I knew. We both traveled way too much and hardly got to see each other, but our bond became so strong that it did not matter how often we got together. We knew if we were needed for a shoulder, a cry or an ear the other was there. Who do you have in your network that could be this shoulder or ear for you when you need them?

CHAPTER 7.

INTUITION IS A SECRET GUIDE

Life is an Audition

Maybe I knew all along not to stop at the *buts*. But why did I? Even as a young tween, wanting to be the next Bruce Springsteen, I knew I'd have to work hard, fall hard, maybe starve to death on my way there—but I stopped at the first hard turn. The flight in the private jet owned by the father of a young up-and-coming band was my first audition after graduating from college. It's one of my most fond memories, but it was also the big but that turned me on my head toward "real jobs."

I announced to my father, who secretly wanted me to win big at this music thing, I had an audition. My father had one of the most incredible voices I've ever heard. His range was nearly a full keyboard, his voice carried our church without a microphone, sitting in the front row always facing the altar and more than five hundred people behind him also singing, my father's voice could be heard loud and clear to the back of the church entrance. People followed him everywhere musically and in our community. He also played trumpet and had an album cut playing trumpet and singing with a big band when he was in his late teens or early twenties. My dad understood the dream, but he feared the path would not allow me enough income to support myself. He was always said, "Have your dream, but you'll need to get a real job so you can eat."

My father, without reluctance and maybe even more curious than me, drove me to a small private airfield on the edge of the southeast edge of Charlotte, North Carolina. As we pulled in, we could see a beautiful private jet coming in for its landing. The excitement was landing inside my heart. We parked the car. Dad and I entered the lobby of the small private airport. A full jungle of butterflies, moths, and bats swelled in my gut, fluttering all over, but I held composure as my dad and I walked over to meet the pilot and his passengers.

We were greeted by what we assumed to be band members wearing suede knee-high lace-up moccasins worn by the younger passengers, and then an older but youthful-looking pilot—who we learned was both the father of the lead guitarist and their financier—wearing newly starched jeans, penny loafers with no socks, white starched button-down shirt, aviator glasses, and dark brown, slicked back Wall Street–style hair—Wall Street meets *GQ* meets rock band.

Maybe this was the first time in my life I really believed I could do anything. Maybe it was the first time I felt my dad's undying desire to support his kids on their journey to reach their dreams, or maybe it was the first time I felt my dad realized he, too, had these big dreams and wanted his kids to achieve theirs'. Either way, this was a pivotal moment in my life. I got on the plane with this band of bros I did not know. My dad seemed to have a faith they were not terrorists after having quizzed the pilot for forty-five minutes. Off we flew to my audition at their private studio, which resided in a city somewhere, but I did not know where.

We were in the air for under two hours. Our jet landed on a private airstrip similar to where we took off. Similar small private planes were rested snug in their hangers or tied down near the small air center. My imagination was running faster than ever as I felt like a newly minted rock star might feel, deplaning for her first-ever diva-to-be concert in a big arena. The pilot/father in front of me, escorting me to the passenger pick-up area, the band members deplaning with me walking around and behind me like my personal bodyguards. They were my entourage. We walked through a small lobby area where other guests and pilots were drinking coffee and chatting then through the front door to the pickup area where a long stretch limo picked us up and off, we went to an area just outside of Nashville! I had no idea that was where I would land when we took off. Funny it never even occurred to me to ask and even funnier, my dad—I would find out later—had more information than I had, which is why he seemed very calm about the whole thing.

At the time it did not matter where I was, how big or famous this band was, or even if I'd ever play with this band in a public venue in my lifetime. It felt like a dream of mine was nearing launch. I imagined it, wrote it in my journal every day for as long as I can remember how I wanted to be a working musician and play music in a band. I had introduced myself as Teresa Ronstadt, after then-famous Linda Ronstadt, or Teresa Springsteen, after the most famous Bruce Springsteen. And here I was, on my way to an audition that could possibly launch this dream into a reality. It was real; I manifested all of this, but I was young and had no idea in my youth the power of my own abilities to create my own realities.

During the thirty-or-forty-minute ride, the band and I got to know each other a little better. My eyes focused on them, but also on the passing beautiful landscapes, quaint little town area, and mansion row of sprawling homes leading into a more industrial office area. We pulled into a parking lot of a large warehouse structure. My nerves were all butterflies meet ax-men kidnappers! We all exited the limo and as I walked into the warehouse the fears exited my body and relief set in, they were a real band! I had never seen such a beautiful rehearsal studio. It occurred to me at the moment I'd never seen any rehearsal studio! And here I am. Now let's get down to business. This band meant business. As we walked in, they quickly introduced me to the other members of the band who'd been waiting for our arrival. I was offered water, juice or soft drinks as the band took their positions. This was fast, too fast, they meant business and had no time to waste and began playing immediately. Did they have other auditions? I do not know. I just knew in the flash of a moment, this dream was no longer my dream. It was their dream!

The audition was a bust! I'd rehearsed many songs they provided me planning for the audition, but they sprung a different song on me in the audition: a Pat Benatar song, "Hit Me with Your Best Shot," *Billboard* magazine's number nine song out of their top one hundred for that time period. UG—the worst of the worst for my voice. Singing Pat Benatar songs was not my range or my raspy, bluesy more female Bruce Springsteen voice. Pat Benatar cover song lead singer I am not! We ran through a few other songs. As we did, I learned a few things about bands in the making that would be recalled throughout my lifetime. While auditioning, I could barely hear myself. I could, however, hear each individual musician in the band playing too loud, runs too long, mics too hot. It wasn't about the band; it was about the individual musician. This band was being driven by individual ego. I could hear each of their egos coming through loud and louder. Instead of realizing my dream, the audition was an epic fail!

The flight back was miserably quiet. I had nothing to say and fought tears back the whole way. Staring out the window of the small jet, it was just the father pilot, copilot, the son band leader, and me. An instant feeling of *I have no future* was gathering in every inch of my body. I ached. I hurt. It was devastating, to say the least. Being a singer and musician had been a dream since I was at least ten years old. That dream had vanished in a Pat Benatar minute. It would take months of sulking and moping around before I would see this one experienced has opened up a door of insight that I treasure even today!

The process of auditioning for this band was an exercise in epic mind shaping. At the ripe old age of twenty-one, I was fresh out of college and ready to attack the world of *choices*! I had to test my intuition. I wondered, *Is it safe to step foot in this little plane and fly away while my father watches his little girl from the tarmac below? Was singing Pat Benatar songs with this band a good choice for me to make? Would this be my one and only chance at performing as the lead singer?* This single episode was my first foray into trusting my instincts and making decisions that would shape the rest of my life.

CHAPTER 8.

STARING IN THE MOVIE OF MY LIFE

We are always auditioning. Interviews for jobs are auditions, seeking venture funding for my start-ups can be a long series of auditions. Being auditioned is even part of being accepted into social clicks and friendship circles. These auditions can feel brutal if we let them, or they can be training camps for what comes next—mental-strength builders for the next big seek!

Venture Seeker

Let me share a time when I'd recently moved from the Northern Virginia area back to my home state of North Carolina. For more than nine years living in Houston, where deals can be done in a sneeze-time, and Northern Virginia, where negotiating deals was an exercise in shared civility. Then, back to my home state of North Carolina, where I returned to business at a snail's pace and where I fell into the founding home of the good ole boy network. Cracking through barriers was something I'd prided myself on but I will say I was not quite prepared for the barrage of challenges I would face trying to get VC funding for a technology start-up as a woman cofounder in the nineties.

I had befriended a venture firm—or individual VC in this firm, Scott—who was very comfortable with my background. He spent time helping me network with start-up founders. I had just left a well-known company, Picturetel. Picturetel was an incredibly successful start-up experience for me—one of the first video-conferencing technology companies and the inventor of compression algorithms for video over the internet. The company grew from $23 million—about the time I had joined them—to over $400 million in less than five years—a big deal at the time.

The company in the late nineties started to downtrend, so I accepted a role as the president of a Dallas-based growing company. This was one of a few true #Metoo experiences. In shock, I stood after having my boob hand-cupped by one of the founders in front of a room full of diners and the company's executive team of our company of which I was president! I abruptly departed the company and took on a contract-consulting project for Intel Corporation.

I spent my entire career forging paths for younger women, especially my daughter, to enter any field. It makes me ill to hear the #Metoo stories still exist and that we're still fighting for equal pay and well-earned titles.

I'll share a few of my personal insights I used on my career path that might have helped my younger self in hopes these secrets can help you.

Don't believe the negative stuff others tell you.

I recently heard the story of a famous woman CEO of a major Fortune 500 media company say she was told she would never make it as a businessperson. She should be a teacher.

Two young professional women were seeking venture capital funding for their start-up. After pitching their start-up, following the pitches of ten male start-ups, the only question the venture capital men in the room asked them was "Could you babysit my kids?"

After getting a job as a business development territory manager at a technology company, I was told on my first day, "Ain't no women yet ever made it in this business, and neither will you!" I achieved the number one salesperson in the entire company. What did my boss do? He proudly announced he had just hired another woman, and *she looked just like me!*

Ladies, these can be debilitating comments that kill the spirit, stop you in your tracks, and mentally exhaust you, *or* you can use comments like these to *fuel* your personal rocket ship to success. You get to choose! I am not saying it will be easy to turn your head, but you do get to choose what you do with this information.

That little voice that yells—screams sometimes—telling you to do something. The voice may start as a soft whisper; then it gets louder and louder, stopping us in our tracks. Listen to all of your voices!

You don't have the experience! You aren't smart enough. Don't say anything; keep this to yourself. Why does no one care? Who cares. But there's no money to do this. It will be hard. No one knows me. If I fail, it will be humiliating. These are not whispers in my head. They are gut-wrenching, knockdown, blowout fights with myself. Do you have these? Whispers are equally halting in moving forward. The subconscious whispers are debilitating: *I am not good enough. I am not worthy. I can't. I won't. I don't know how.* Whatever is going on in that brain is a fight. It can take over your body and create too much anxiety. These voices make you sick. They have only one true good purpose and that is to keep us safe when in danger. They may whisper, "Watch out—this guy has got an agenda", or "This gal's a bit manipulative." But when the voices in your head take over your mind, body, soul and spirit the voices take over and control every step we take—or don't take, as the case may be—and we lose control of our own lives.

What is a person to do? Yoga, mindfulness, meditation! Yes, these are all good; they quiet down and often completely shoot down these voices. However, when the monsters want to, they jump out and scare the hell out of you, mostly when you least expect it. Managing these voices is not easy; they will not completely go away. But you can quiet them, use these voices as lessons. I found, as many of you may have, getting up early, and write every morning. Get all that crappy stuff out of my head and on to the paper can be like drinking a colonic cleanse. The more I write, and sometimes the faster I allow the words to come out, the more relief I feel. The paper becomes a punching bag of sorts, where I can punch out these debilitating thoughts, work out the fears, calm the anxiety, and even create my own horror script, where I am the victim at the mercy of evil people, and then literally rip the paper out of my journal and throw it in the fire to burn for no one to read.

Some kind of calm and peace come over me when I write each morning and I am ready for the day's decisions. Big risks don't feel as big, challenging problems tend to feel less challenging. My stalled creativity turns into the roaring fire burning up the pages I just wrote. Now I'm ready for a day of creating! And I am ready for tackling what the world throws at me.

CHAPTER 9.

REALITY IS NOT ALWAYS WHAT YOU SEE

It was such a sobering event, walking through a funeral home to help my father pick out a coffin for my uncle. This was my first time in a funeral home having to consider the business of death. My father was a quiet contemplative man. When he spoke you either laughed hysterically because everything was funny or you stopped everything you were doing to listen to his brilliance. He spent years caring for my mom's brother unconditionally. From both my mom and my dad, I learned what unconditional love really meant. They gave us their undivided attention. They dedicated themselves to their church and to their community. They gave where and what they could of themselves; their time was other people's time. My parents worked hard to support our family, all the while handing out food and clothing to people in need. They were always giving. My reality was one of giving. Seeing life for what it is but to never assume anything. My dad was incredible at seeing the reality underneath what you could not see.

Back to this trip with my father to the funeral home. We walked from the front office to the back showroom to pick out a coffin for my uncle. As we walked, my dad and I notice an open casket with a young something women lying peacefully. I'd experienced death with older members of my family but viewing this young woman took my breath away, kicking me in the gut extremely hard, I could hardly hold a heavy cry back. My father's eyes closed for a moment as if in deep prayer for her. We slowed our pace out of respect and then entered the room with all the caskets. This is a sobering event for anyone that has never been through preparations of burying or memorializing a close relative or friend. We selected a simple casket, which I learned is not: a. Simple, b. Not just the casket but the vault that the casket goes into to protect the body inside. What? There were many other options and to me these options were mind-blowingly nuts. But I have learned burials and funerals are more for the living to help us grieve and to know we've done all we could for our loved ones.

We completed our selections and turned to walk back to the office. I stopped for a second to gather myself before walking by the receiving room where the beautiful young woman lay ready to greet her receivers. Tears already are streaming down my cheeks as we started the path toward where she lay resting. I held my breath, glanced over nearly passing out as this young woman *sat up*! She freaking sat straight up, climbed out of the casket, and walked away!

I choked! Did my dad see this? He was behind me and had not entered the receiving area yet. She was gone, the casket was empty. My dad and the funeral director were deep in conversation as they walked to his office. He never looked over at the casket and I followed them holding a blend of laughter and tears in as best as I could. I could barely get the word out. Yes, I agree when asked a question. I looked all around. The woman never appeared. I casually strolled around the home, waiting for my dad to finish, but never saw her again. When we got in the car, I started laughing very hard and told my dad what I saw. This to be one of our saddest days turned into one of the funniest things I'd ever seen and we both were uncontrollably laughing. Was this young woman an angel? Was she testing the coffin out for herself or for a loved one? Was she taking a nap?

I'd assumed death, cancer maybe, heart attack, or a rare disease took her life. I'd assumed every possible scenario but the ones that may have been real. She was either taking a nap or testing the coffin out. I guess she was also an angel, teaching me one of life's most valuable lessons! Never assume anything! Ask fierce questions; seek out the honest truth of the matter, because what seems obvious is rarely truth!

These are valuable lessons in business and in life:

1. Never assume anything: ask questions, get specific, make sure you hear correctly what others are saying, and ensure they too are hearing and can repeat what you are asking of them or saying.

2. Don't take things for granted: this goes hand in hand with never assume anything. Don't take for granted things are going well. Make sure you do your due diligence daily, weekly and monthly. Mistakes happen but the more you keep your finger on the pulse of the business measures and have double and triple checks on those metrics the more you squeeze the risk of taking things for granted and then being caught off guard.

3. Your eyes may tell you one thing but upon a deeper look you see the truth. No, I would have never walked over to the casket to see if she was alive. My eyes told me, because that is the only association I have with someone lying in a casket, that she was dead. Eyes can deceive so dig deeper and seek out the best version of the truth.

CHAPTER 10.

THE "HEAD" AT THE TABLE

Your Head

What goes on in your head when you sit quietly listening to the voices around the room? What about while sitting in a conference room discussing new ideas, a decision that needs to be made or whether to fire or keep someone. Are you tuned in to your body? Is your gut in knots, your chest squeezing the breath out of you? Are you sweating?

Maybe you have a private dialogue in your head that needs to become part of the discussion around the table. What's holding you back from speaking your mind, your truth or sharing your ideas?

This is one of the most personal challenges individuals face in their professional careers. How and when do I raise issues or my ideas?

The Multiplier Effect
versus
the Diminisher Effect!

On numerous occasions, I have stepped in as an interim CEO or taken a leadership role to client companies with the goal to turnaround some challenging situation. When challenges like these happen in companies, the emotions begin to run hot and not in a good way. Revenues are down, stresses are at an all-time high, customers are leaving and/or complaining that services are awful and a feeling of helplessness often sets in.

Worse, the best talent leaves the company in droves, creating big holes to fill during some of the toughest times. On top of that, the challenged leadership has become unnerved. They have no idea the impact they are creating and the uncertainty they are causing for everyone else. What was once a healthy culture begins to turn sour.

First, you must know you can rebound from these challenging times. Second, nearly every start-up company goes through tough times. Third, people can make all the difference in the world to get through the roughest of times. Let me share an example of one of my personal experiences. There are many takeaways to learn from this experience, but I will share just a few:

I was in a meeting with our team and the founder of the company. The team shared an important decision on a topic from the previous week's meeting. They had been told it was their choice as a team to make. As they shared the decision and the plan of action, the temperature in the room immediately dropped. The founder expressed, harshly, "This was not the decision I ordered!" Steam continued to build, along with insults, demands, and inconsiderate slurs from the founder's mouth. I've never heard such a string of uncalled for, ugly, hateful, and demeaning words. Somehow a new era of company culture was defining itself right in front of me. It felt like a freight train that was out of control. The more you called time out, the hotter the individual got.

The team completely shut down, eyes rolled to the back of heads, and a feeling of complete defeat for doing the right thing overcame everyone. I felt sad for two reasons: One) that I could not stop this from doing damage, and two) for the people in the room who were dedicated to this individual. They were disillusioned. Things quickly became personal, with blame for not following direct orders shooting out like bullets to the heart.

Sadly, I have been there before! I know in the moment it's hard to rationalize with someone out of control in the midst of their tantrum. In many cases, this individual is unaware of their own power, the good it can lead to, or the negative repercussions it fuels. I understand how it must feel to be informed of being let go for not doing what one is told to do. It is tumultuous when great people are glorified, being complimented one minute but then smacked on the back of the head and made to feel lesser of themselves the next minute. It makes anyone feel like shitt. Worse, it paralyzes people.

I call this the diminisher effect! Diminisher effects completely shut off the flow of potential creative genius. It closes the door for any opportunity of a "magnifier effect" which elevates people and productivity to its highest.

Bully bosses are sly little devils. You may not know you have one until it's too late. If you live in constant anxiety, are experiencing a void of great ideas, or worse, you don't recognize who you are any longer, you just may have a bully boss or a leader who only encourages diminishing returns from his or her people.

Signs You Need to Change Bosses, Transfer, or Change Jobs:

1. Anxieties are high for you and/or the organization.

2. You never know where you stand. You are celebrated one minute and punished the next minute.

3. There is no eye contact when talking to this person; they avoid it.

4. You feel undermined by your boss or more than one person.

5. You are asked to do a special project, but when you report on the project there is no recognition of ever assigning you that project.

6. Your boss or company holds things over your head. For example, you got that increase you asked for, and they were able to justify it by the results you have proven to gain. But every day you are threatened with having the new increase taken from you for no reason.

7. You were invited to the company party and came, but stayed only a short time, now you are feeling the pressure that you are not a team player and you are told everyone noticed that you left early.

8. Too many of your conversations start with "You are ...." Followed by what feels like a ding. "Too honest, too trusting, too nice, too creative, too quiet ..."

   a. Before turning these to negatives in your head, try to qualify them with the boss or individual calling you out on your *toos*. For example:

- What do you mean by this?
- How is this affecting my work here?
- Help me with what positive effect you feel this attribute has on my work.
- How does this relate to our key performance objectives?

b. As you work to understand the positives, the person delivering these statements only leans to negatives. It may be time for a transfer or time to change companies.

These all can create powerful feelings, causing great anxiety and undue stress. If you feel you are somehow experiencing these, don't immediately jump to "It's my boss," or "It's the company's fault." Seek out some coaching or advice to help you work through the challenges. All start-ups experience anxious times, but dealing with toxic bosses or cultures is not healthy for anyone.

EXERCISE 5—EMOTION JOURNALING

It is up to each person to recognize his or her true preferences.

—*Isabel Briggs Meyers*

To understand what triggers your emotions, good or otherwise, it is important to write in the very moment you first feel your stomach churn, or your eyebrows sweat. Keep a small notebook or a journal with you at all times. As nutty as it sounds, I use to tie a small ribbon around my arm or a finger to act as a reminder, which would make me more aware of my emotions at all times.

1. Keep a daily emotions journal.

    a. Before you go to work, log in your journal how you feel in the morning. Write about how you feel while you have your coffee and morning quiet time. Keep track of your emotions prior to going to work. Is there a shift from calm to anxiousness when you put your coat on and start to leave? Write it down!

    b. Write in your journal how you feel at lunch, how you feel when you get home, documenting your emotions throughout the day is an important part of this exercise. Discover what is triggering these emotions?

c. Keep this journal at a minimum for thirty days.

2. Check-in on your emotional journal for what are the consistent themes. Are you filled with joy and happiness most of the journal or are you feeling good in the morning? Then as soon as you have your first interaction, what is triggered in your body to make you feel anxious, stressed, angry or upset?

    a. Use these uncomfortable or unwanted feelings to learn! This is a time when self-awareness is key to personal growth. Leverage a personal development program, hire a coach, and seek out some reading materials on self-growth. You may also take an assessment for self-awareness. Here is one example: Meyers Briggs is one of the most popular tools to learn more about your personality type. Are you very emotional and your feelings get hurt easily? Are you intuitive, judgmental? You can learn more about how Meyers Briggs works by researching more here: https://www.myersbriggs.org.

3. Once you have taken the first two steps you are ready to begin building an action plan for change. Are you developing yourself more in ways that strengthen areas you want to work on? Are you developing an action plan for leaving your job as the culture or company no longer fits into your personal plan? These are healthy ways to

tackle change in your life. This method will serve you as it puts you in control of your life versus blaming others for where you are.

JOURNALING 101

Why is journaling so important? Why do I use journaling in each of the seventeen lessons?

Journaling what is on our minds clears our minds for new things. Writing our frustrations, writing about how angry we feel, and digging into why we feel that anger can be a strong part of a healing process.

The more we write, the more room there will be for fresh perspectives. Emptying the clutter of monkey-mind onto pages of paper is freeing. With each writing, you dig a little deeper. I have journals for ideas; I have journals for capturing feelings and emotions, which I throw away when filled up; I have journals for business; and I have journals for personal thoughts.

Writing helps to uncover the root cause of frustration and the root of great happiness. By documenting these daily thoughts, feelings and expressions over time you may find your creative juices flowing like a beautiful stream. The more you practice journaling the more uncertainty may melt away.

There are no rules to journaling, just write. Noted in Julia

Cameron's best-selling book, *The Artist Way*, writing three pages in the morning—morning pages—with great discipline helps your day get started with a clearer mind

> *Pages clarify our yearnings. They keep an eye on our goals. They may provoke us, coax us, comfort us, even cajole us, as well as prioritize and synchronize the day at hand. If we are drifting, the pages will point that out. They will point the way True North. Each morning, as we face the page, we meet ourselves. The pages give us a place to vent and a place to dream. They are intended for no eyes but our own.*
> —Julia Cameron, **The Miracle of Morning Pages**

CHAPTER 11.

LEADERS – I THOUGHT I UNDERSTOOD

Sometimes when you least expect it you sit still and realize, you are *so lost*. Have you ever wondered what the fuck did I just go through? And why! How did I not see this coming? Wait—I actually predicted this outcome, yet I did nothing to protect myself from getting sucked in.

Getting caught up in the tornado of bullying, stress, and manipulation is not hard to do.

CONTROL THE HYPE

When do you get lost in the hype? Lost in the hype of what? For example, when people disagree, yet they are saying the same thing. When do the voices start to rise to a feverous pitch, so much so it sounds like arguing for the sake of being right, yet now one is right? The heat in the room is high, and no one seems to be listening. Some are yelling, and there are right piles everywhere. Everyone has enough Google research to make themselves right! I call these "right piles." We can all be right, but if you get lost in the hype and do not gain collaboration or consensus, everyone risks being incredibly wrong. The tension in the room feels worse to you than being wrong. The tension, the emotional outbreaks feel childish, senseless and manipulative. This is getting lost in the hype!

Fill in this blank: I get lost in the hype when_____.

Is the hype possibly emotional outbreaks or pointing fingers, accomplishing nothing that was asked of you, or so someone says?

Is your hype that you don't accept the status quo of emotional outrages?

Consider what's real.

Consider what's fake.

Are you going to work to succeed at all costs, getting lost in the hype? What are those costs? Health, doubting oneself, etc.

People need predictability! They need hope, dreams, and purpose.

Stop the Screams and Chaos.

Stop Feeding the lions and watch for the lambs.

Stop!

I've found there is little middle ground with entrepreneurial leaders. They are either lions or lambs. Sometimes us leaders are lions dressed up in lamb fur on the rare occasion there are lambs masking themselves as lions. In the vein of authenticity, a word used way too often without authentic actions, showing up as who you really are is important.

Could we be lucky enough to get what you see and see what you get? Do we revel in the opportunity to work with strong charismatic leaders? Do we see and understand the lions and lambs? Somewhere in a strong leader's experience—maybe it's in their DNA—certain individuals are naturally born as great leaders and you are lucky to enjoy such a positive experience. More, your own leadership style may grow from their positive leadership style.

For those who have the opposite of the above: remember, it's all temporary, and every experience contributes to our growth journey.

Often the lion leader's roar is just too loud, too wrong, too harmful. And ultimately pointless.

Hear Them Roar

You hear the lions roar! You want to tame this beast, but how? You work three times harder trying to please the lion working to keep your job secure. You never quite hit their happy place with your work, though. Often the lion seems to pit two people against each other to tackle the same goal. You learn this halfway through a special project when you run into a workmate only to find out they were given the same directive. What the F! Should you continue? Is your job on the line? Did I do something wrong? You begin to question yourself. Self-doubt consumes your body. The lion's roar only gets louder, maybe even turns ugly because the lion is never satisfied! Lion's appetites are rarely satisfied! What do you do? How do you navigate this lion boss?

What Did You Say?

I once had a boss who whispered in every executive leadership meeting. He favored me for some reason. He said I reminded him of his sister. He always sat next to me in meetings. I could hear everything he said, but others in the room, especially on conference calls, were always politely asking, "Could you repeat that, Andy?"

Then he would turn to me and repeat it in a way that only I could hear. And I would repeat it for him more loudly. Why do this? It was a tactic of his. Strange as it may sound this was a lion in a lamb's suit! Andy would often issue a directive or project for the leadership team to take action on. Everyone on the team collaborated on the directive. We proudly report on progress in the next meeting. Our lion in a lamb's suit slowly turned to me, and I quote: "Why the hell is everyone wasting time on this?"

Quietly manipulative, calculating, playing on our psyches to challenge him, yet we took him literally and didn't push back. But I knew this about him and learned not to compromise my strong leadership values to compensate for his way of leading. Instead I strengthened my own leadership skills and realized what did not work for me as an individual. Not saying this is easy. To survive and learn how to thrive with that type of culture is critical. I was determined that I'd do what was right for me. Let the chips fall where they may. I will be true to myself.

The lamb can be tricky. You feel they are genuine and clear when in reality our little lamb never says what he or she means. When they give one directive but mean something completely different a directive goes unmet. You, however, feel you did what you were asked. What the heck just happened? How do I navigate this every day?

Know it's not personal! Don't take it personally. We are learning more about ourselves on a journey of life. Lions and lambs are everywhere in our lives, not just our work or our bosses. What can you do to strengthen you on leadership style and build better more collaborative relationships?

Exercise 6—Lion or Lamb

I was not the lion, but it fell to me to give the lion's roar.

—*Winston Churchill*

Create a leadership journal. If you haven't gotten this yet, journals are a very important part of a strong growth process for reaching the goals in life that we want.

1. Every day write the best and the worst leadership styles you have experienced at work with your boss and/or team members. Also, capture what you perceive as good leadership skills in others you come in contact with. Maybe it's your waiter at a restaurant, or maybe it's a politician you love or do not care for. What is it about their style, their works, their facial expressions and body language that you like, and what do you not care for?

2. On another page, write your leader style intentions. What are the three to five main character traits you want to develop and hold yourself accountable!

3. Build a progress chart and monitor your progress on developing and using your traits.

4. Ask a trusted friend to help.

5.   Ask for feedback and document this feedback. In my work we call these tiny or micro-goals and pulsing others for feedback on developing these goals is valuable feedback. Do others feel you are improving in these areas? Feedback is a critical part of all growth plans.

CHAPTER 12.

THE WAY FORWARD: THE BEGINNING

My path has been filled with a wide diversity of opportunities none of which I mapped out or planned ahead of time. An idea would spark inside of me after reading an article or two in a magazine. For those not used to paper, that was all we had! I loved to read everything I could get my hands on about business, technology, trends. It's a passion of mine and in part a creative endeavor. Technology was altering the state of the arts even when I was in my early twenties, and I found it fascinating.

When I graduated from college there were few jobs. I did anything I could to make a living. I watered plants and washed windows of businesses, I worked in retail—for one week and quit—and I worked as a fitness instructor and manager of a Fitness Center. I sold memberships, taught fitness classes and kept up the books for the one center I worked for until I realized there was something funky about how they were paying people or not paying their employees as they should. It was a lesson learned very early in my working life. Do I keep this to myself and just keep working? Do I report it and get fired, or do I report it and quit? It was not a hard decision, as my father's moral code was in my ear and with his help and confirmation something was not quite right. I reported it and quit, never looking back.

From there I jumped to working for an engineering firm during the day and started bartending and singing/playing guitar at a globally known hotel at night. It felt like twenty-two hours of work and two hours of sleep per day, but I did not mind the work. I actually enjoyed the very different dynamics of the work learning what I could about people. One day two police officers walked into our offices of my day job and handed the owner papers. He was being sued by companies for not paying his bills. Another dilemma presented itself: Do I leave, or do I continue to work and help him get back on his feet?

This was a small company. After they'd won several million-dollar contracts, the founder's early partner decided that he didn't want to share a partnership anymore. Without any discussion, he went into the office one night very late, stealing blueprints, contract documents, and other paperwork. He proceeded to try hard to take business from his now former partner's company. It was a devastating set of events no one ever plans for, expects to happen, or wants to happen. They were college friends, good buddies, and had handshake deals to build this business.

I stayed with the founder to help keep the business going, and it ended up being a life-changing set of events for me. Not only did I do the marketing, but I sported a tool belt and built alongside the engineering team process control panels, learning engineering concepts as each panel was designed and built. I was sent along with one of the executive engineers to a major tea company to install a process control panel in their manufacturing facility. Me, twenty-one years old, sporting a tool belt. Not an engineer by education but learning engineering concepts on the job. Walking over to the panel, which was the size of semitruck and trailer, ready to install this panel. The control panel would be running the entire manufacturing operation! On the one hand, I felt honored that my company had faith in me that I could do this installation of a panel I helped to build. On the other hand, the VP of engineering at the tea company manufacturing facility was about ready to call ranks and get me out of there. On yet another hand the company I worked for had little options but to have me performing this installation. They needed to get themselves back into financial health.

End of story: I installed the panel successfully. The VP of

engineering of the tea company came over to shake my hand and congratulate me for what I later learned was doing the job only a man could or should do. The company regained its financial health and was acquired. I applied to a radio station for a job in sales, thinking this would be a great way to make money and learn something new. I was accepted as an account representative at a major radio station in Winston-Salem, North Carolina. This would end up being one of the best jobs ever to help my career trajectory take off into a new stratosphere. I had now progressed from engineer to selling air time for a radio station.

The radio station had just been acquired by a Fortune 500 insurance company. They were investing in building a broadcast franchise of TV and radio stations. I consider this time in my work history one of the most valuable times of my career. This company invested thousands of dollars in training and development for its employees. I loved the training, I loved the job, and I loved the people I worked with. My bosses invested time and training in us on their own as well. Not just technical radio-speak training but real professional development. They understood the more value and insights we could bring to our customers the more successful the station would be, earning and keeping long term advertisers.

Each job presented its own unique set of growth challenges, I had to learn to navigate around many obstacles, beliefs, behaviors—you name it. There was the multimedia production company where I learned that the CEO's mother was the receptionist, and she guarded all marketing material with her life, not allowing anyone to just hand out brochures because they cost too much to print, which made my job much more difficult. In order to prepare for any meetings with senior executives the CEO's mom wanted to talk to her son. Her son traveled weeks at a time and she did not want to bother him with phone calls. An interesting time for sure.

Then there was the optical imaging technology company where. If you recall, in a prior chapter, I shared how on my first day a man walked up to my cubicle and said, "Ain't no woman made it yet in this business, and you will not either!" I ignored the comments and went on to be the number one salesperson out of 240 men and less than 4 women. My boss, thrilled with my accomplishments and the fact that he hired me, proudly introduced me to a new hire—another woman—and he said, 'She looks just like you." He knew she would also be successful. "She looks just like you," he kept saying.

For the most part, I ignored these comments. Maybe because of the incredible faith my father had in me to be successful at anything I really wanted to do in life, or maybe because my five brothers treated me no different than they treated each other, except the fact that *I was the football* much of the time! I really never went looking for validation from anyone. I always worked to better myself to do the best that I could and learn the most that I could then move on to the next big thing. Sometimes actions or statements stung, but I had my eyes on a bigger picture even though my canvas was not painted yet.

In my early twentiess, my first few jobs could not have been more different or disconnected. For me it was all about the new directions, new technologies, and anything new that excited me. I wanted to get involved and learn what I could. That was the case when I left the optical imaging company, which was on a downward spin for a new little start-up technology company out of Boston. I was living in Houston, Texas, the state of *big*—big squirrels, big roaches, big men, big hair, big meals, and big hearts! Everything was just incredibly big.

I found a company I really wanted to work for and set out to get a job with them. I submitted resumes. I contacted the executives in Boston. I resent resumes. I continued to call the executives in Boston writing letters, calling and just committed myself to getting a job with this new company. I had no experience in the technology. There was no reason for them to talk to me. I had very few of the experiences they posted for hires. The company was one of the top three venture-funded video conferencing companies in the world and was starting to gain some press after going IPO. I continued my outreach even though I never got any acknowledgment of my communications. About a year after I started my quest to work for this company, I got a message that the regional director was looking to hire a regional sales representative in Texas, and they would like to talk with me. I nearly fell over!

After a phone interview, the regional director agreed to fly me in to meet with him and interview a second time. The interview went very well, but my experience was not in this industry, more senior and experienced people were candidates and my contacts were not going to do me any good. I knew the regional director felt I was a great candidate, but he was torn. After not hearing back for a week, I called the director and he told me they chose another candidate! Something possessed me at that moment and I said very strongly "No! I am a great candidate; do not hire him. I will fly myself out to you and give me one more chance to prove I can do this job!"

The director was quiet for what felt like twenty minutes but was more like fifteen seconds. He said, "No, don't spend your money. I will fly to you." He did. He hired me, and I did not let him down.

Lessons from the Beginning and the Middle

You are the master of your universe—don't let other's dictate what you are or are not capable of doing. If you want it but are denied, find another way to go after it. Maybe your job skills and experience are holding you back from reaching that dream job. Find something that may provide you with the experience you need. I thought I wanted to sell surgical equipment to hospitals for a division of a major medical equipment manufacturer in my early twenties. But despite them loving me and telling me I was a great fit—wait for it—"We just don't know what to do with your hair." Back then companies could say these things, they could hire or not hire someone based on a certain look—and they did.

Many things prepared me for tackling some very tough times in my life. I never make light of looking back at these memories. They allowed me to make some of the best in-the-moment decisions that would make or break my career. Now let me share a few of my stories in the hopes you will not feel alone in the most embarrassing moments of your life.

Where is the Door?

Growth comes with the oddest of circumstances. For example, doors are often taken for granted, yet they open up into a whole new world of experiences.

Be an opener of doors.

—*Ralph Waldo Emerson*

I was offered a role to lead the North American headquarters of a Norwegian start-up software company. The company was VC funded. The first order of business to get started was to spend several weeks in Norway. I was looking forward to my travels, as I'd never been to Norway but knew it would be a beautiful scenic trip with what little time I had to explore.

A very important aspect of working globally is to do the best you can to understand the culture, not just how business is done but of the people in the region. As I often do, I brush up on my cultural understanding. I bought a great little travel book on Norway and its culture at the airport before departing for the long journey. During my reading, I found several notations concerning doors in Norwegians homes and businesses and how Norwegians liked their walls flush and the doors often blend into the walls. You may not always see evidence of a door. I read this with a passing interest and moved on to the following chapters finishing the book before arriving for my connecting flight through Oslo.

Rushing through Oslo, Norway, to catch my connecting flight, I found a small section of restrooms, each with private doors, and rushed in one. As I turned away from the sink after washing my hands, I grabbed my roller suitcase and briefcase, took one step toward the door handle and felt an instant twist of my shoe sliding out from under me and up in the air my legs, my briefcase and my arms go and slamming down on the hard white tiled floor with my head first knocking so hard I felt my stomach rolling up into my throat. Not sure if I was going to pass out, throw up, die right there in a private restroom where *no one* could hear or see or find me, I just simply laid still for a few moments. Flashing through my mind: Will I ever see my family again? Do I have a concussion? Did I break anything in my body? Will I ever see my family again? No one will ever find me in here.

OK. First, this is not my door story! I will continue that story in a moment. The pain in my head turned from dizzying to pounding. I was to the point of nearly passing out. I slowly got up, held my breath for a few seconds, again, thinking I was going to throw up and/or pass out. Recovering my composure and my gut, I gathered my things and meekly slid out of the restroom and began walking to my next flight. Once I was safely on my connecting flight to Trondheim, I wrote some revelations in my journal, which is like a part of my body—it goes everywhere with me:

1. When traveling alone, especially in a foreign country, never use a private restroom in a far corner of an airport where you are pretty sure no one ever investigates or sees for weeks at a time.

2. Always have an emergency plan. A beacon of sorts or today cell phones that are enabled for emergency calls for the country you are in.

3. Ensure your loved ones have your itinerary. Keep them up to date on any changes to that itinerary.

4. Carry with you a first aid kit. These can be very small and fit easily in a briefcase.

5. That all the lessons above go toward entrepreneurial emergencies. Very often the stresses of being an entrepreneur can cause anxiety attacks, depression, very strong highs, and extremely low lows. All too often founders are not prepared for the metaphorical falls that feel deadly or knock the breath out of you. *Preparation* and *anticipation* are very important.

And Now for the Door!

The flight from Oslo to Trondheim was very short. Our approach must have been one of the more beautiful approaches I'd ever seen. Snowcapped mountains deep in their winter sleep, the Norwegian Sea—I would come to learn my office was on the water and faced the seaside—and cotton-candy clouds. Sunrays streamed in through the window, setting up for a beautiful sunset. The flight landed on the tarmac. It's the last flight of the day coming into this little airport.

There may have been twenty of us on the flight now walking from the stairs of the plane to the tarmac to walk into the arrival and luggage claim area. Thinking it would take a few minutes for them to unload our checked baggage I jump into a restroom to check my head for big knots from my earlier fall, check my hair and face to make sure I look presentable as the founder to the Norwegian company will be there to greet me on the other side of the baggage claim area door. I walk out of the restroom, look around and realize I am *completely alone*, me and my bag sitting in the middle of this small baggage area. And there is no door! I do a 360, completely disoriented. No one to check and stamp my passport. This is shortly after September 11, 2001, mind you, when global airport security was at its peak. No door! There are no people, there is no door, there is no way out that I can see.

For a brief moment I felt panicky. This was the last flight of the day. I'd only jumped in the restroom for less than a minute and out to find that the airport had closed up and left me all alone. Gathering my composure, again, I remembered my little travel book section talking about the doors in some Norwegian buildings and homes being flush with the walls nearly invisible. I slowly moved to the edges of the room and ran my hand over the wall all around the room. Nothing! Once more I slowly walked the edges of the room and stopped briefly, wondering if this was it for me for the night. At that moment two walls slid open into what looked like an alternate universe. On the other side of a short corridor was a glass atrium waiting area were two gentlemen smiling big Norwegians smiles stood ready to greet the lost little puppy I was. Relief!

My perspective on business and life shifted at that moment. The doors of Norway opened much more than just the entry to their beautiful country, incredible culture, beautiful landscapes, and wonderful people. It opened my mind to what possibilities am I not seeing because they are just not visible or obvious. Hold this thought as we will come back to it.

Midtrip, a few days after our company's board meeting, I was asked to join the chairman for dinner. I assumed the CEO or others would join us, but no, it was just the chairman and me. Not thinking any more about the dinner, I enjoyed a leisure walk from my office on the walkways by the water to my hotel to get ready for dinner.

We ordered drinks and chatted about the state of the business and opportunities ahead of us; then we ordered the evening's special salmon dinner and continued talking about trends in the industry. Our nice chat continued, as does my suspicion. There was more to come than the niceties of our dinner conversation. We ordered tea and coffee and a light pastry dessert. I noticed little beads of sweat forming on his brows and finally asked if there were any further important considerations I needed to know before contributing to driving the business forward.

He stops, puts his coffee cup down and says, "I want you to sell this company and recoup the investors' funds." Wait, what? He went on to say—this is still in my first week, mind you—the CEO was being removed, and he'd like me to help him lead the company and assist him in selling the company as quickly as possible. The investors had lost patience with:

1. the misrepresentation of hitting the revenue goals,

2. the CEO spending too much too fast and not focused enough, and

3. the CEO's travels were "out of control" and not focused and were not contributing to the business goals.

Mind you, it's now nearing midnight, and he's still sharing details of the reorganization and what they'd really brought me on to do and how they were very excited about the prospects about me selling the business and them recouping their investments. As he's talking, I feel as though in this far from home country I've just fallen again, hit my head on the marble floor, dizzily got up but couldn't find any doors to let me out!

One door closes and an unexpected unseen door opens to a whole new world!

SHOE MATTERS AND THE SLIP THAT SLIPPED

As I did most mornings while living and working in Reston, Virginia, I put my workout clothes on in the dark to not wake my husband or six-year-old daughter. I packed up my gym bag and gathered my work clothes to change into after the gym workout. Workouts and exercise have always been a staple in my life. Working out wakes up my brain, keeps my energy level up, and helps with my mental agility. It's food for me!

On this particular morning, I finished my workout and dressed for work. I reach into my bag for my shoes only to find I have packed two different shoes: one black shoe with a two-inch heel and one Mary Jane blue-and-red shoe with a three-inch heel! Looking at my watch, my heart thumps faster and faster. I was running late for an important speaking engagement, and I had no time to run home. It was time to set a new fashion trend.

Two Different Shoes:

Two Valuable Options!

I turned my potential shoe fiasco into a story of two-valued options that new technologies I was presenting could bring to the audience I was speaking to. Instead of stopping in my tracks, in two different shoes, I found a way to flip this disaster on its head and use it to my advantage. Was it comfortable? No! Was I shaking and very nervous inside? Did these thoughts of, *You nut—this is horrible*! go through my mind the whole time I am up there? Was I sweating? Yes! A big yes! Did I have any other options? Sure, I could have canceled, could have asked someone to step in, could have done a lot of things, but at the moment I felt being creative could work to my advantage. Maybe it would lighten the room and be a fresh approach to the corporate blue suits. After all, this was the time of the corporate gray-and-blue suit. It was risky as a sense of humor that was required for times like this, but I was willing to take the risk. It all worked out.

The Slip

Many of my younger readers may not even know what a slip is, but I will explain. I worked for a technology company in my very early thirties that was in the midst of reinventing themselves. This was one of the companies I spoke of previously, where on my first day I was told, "Ain't no woman yet made it in this business." Two years into it, having been awarded top sales accolades, I got pregnant with my first child. Women in technology were rare at the time, and being a pregnant woman in technology was even rarer. I made it work for the company and for me as I really enjoyed the work. My boss's wife worked in technology so he greatly appreciated me and also was very supportive in mentoring me.

I felt great throughout my pregnancy and worked up till the week I was due. Two weeks before my due date I had scheduled a demonstration and executive presentation in our offices to five senior officers of one of the largest banks in the country. I had successfully proposed a solution to the company of our technology. We were narrowed as one of the top two choices. Our competitor had already had this company in for an executive briefing. I knew we must have them in before I left for maternity leave. It simply could not wait. This deal would be one of the largest deals my company had ever won if it all went well.

I am nine months pregnant, big as a house, and I dress in a white maternity dress. That was the only thing I felt was executively presentable enough. Because it was white and I would be standing to present to the group I wanted something underneath my skirt to be sure you could not see lines of my maternity undies. A *slip*! A white half-slip, I had one, but it was a bit tight around my baby bump. I cut a few incisions in the elastic just enough to feel comfortable but still fitted around my waist. I am ready, I feel great, my boss complimented me on looking terrific and glowy, and we were ready.

We are in the conference room. My boss, my boss's boss, and five senior executives of the largest bank in the country, all men. I have spent more than an hour sharing my presentation and just about to demonstrate our product to the group. I get up and walk to our large optical imaging technology unit to demonstrate the unit. I lift my arms with great exaggeration to show the technology device's features. I am about to demonstrate when my boss points to me, eyes wide open, face white as a sheep and subtly points down to my feet. I glance down, horrified. My white slip had fallen and was wrapped around my ankles.

Breathe, breathe, breathe. I turned beet red. My boss said, "What are you going to do with that thing?" I immediately kicked up my slip, tossed it in my hands, and then throw it to one of the bank executives, who caught it and looked at me to see if he should laugh hysterically or cry!

Then, out of my possessed mouth, came the words, "Now that we've slipped through that unanticipated problem, what do you say? Sign our contract now, because you know we can handle any crisis as they come up. You can see we are quick to respond!" Surprising me and my boss, *they bought*! After a bout of historical laughter!

EXERCISE 7: PLANNING FOR UNANTICIPATED CIRCUMSTANCES

You may find this exercise challenging, but I assure you it will be valuable. Anticipating challenges and outcomes that you do not expect is not easy in life or in your start-up. I am also here to tell you every time you start a new company the challenges are different. Maybe you get better at anticipating what could go wrong, but it will feel different in every company you start. How best can you anticipate challenges? Here are some strategies to help.

1. Got that journal out? Get some different color pens and use the pen color that best reflects your emotions as you write the exercise steps below.

2. Now write.
    a. What is the worse imaginable thing that could happen to your business?

        i. Run out of funds?
        ii. Lose your top customer?
        iii. A business partner passes away unexpectedly
        iv. Business partners want out of the business, and they want you to buy them out, and you say, "With what?

    b. For each of the above, write out an outlined action plan as to what you would do.

    c. For example: Let's say you have a business partner who dies unexpectedly without a will or key man insurance to protect the company what do you do?

All challenges are survivable. My clients and I have survived many disasters without anticipating them. Why not plan and consider what you would do if these happen to you or your business. You will be better prepared to deal with them.

EXERCISE 8: WHAT-IF GAME

This is a great game to play. What-ifs may turn serious, but it's a great way to plan for the unanticipated. One thing to keep in mind that good news and opportunities unanticipated can turn not great if you are not ready and prepared for them.

An example of this might be: What if we had a customer that wanted your business to take on five times more than your normal business with this client? What resources would you need to add? What would it do to your current operations? What pressures would it add to your business or what resources would it take away from your current customer base?

1. What if we got three times the additional business than we have currently overnight?

2. What if we lose our top paying customer?

3. What if our most valuable team members were to leave the company?

4. What if we cannot source new hires as quickly as we need them?

5. What if our technology is no longer relevant?

These are examples of anticipated what-ifs. Doing this exercise frequently may help you and your team overcome challenges more quickly by being better prepared. Answering takes time and should be repeated for this to be a valuable exercise!

CHAPTER 13.

RAGS TO RICHES TO RAGS AND THEN?

Yep, this is me. The rise to riches was stressful, very hard work—years and years of work. It was also a time of intense focus on feeding my inner entrepreneurial spirit and at the same time it was an amazing, fun, engaging ride, for the most part, doing meaningful work.

On the path to search-for the next big trends, a bit of search for self opens us up to the possibilities. It's part of the formula for making "lucky" find you. I was lucky, but I feel I created a lot of my luck by seeking opportunities out with a deep line of questioning, curiosity, and connections.

For sure the ride up to luck can be a bit anxiety ridden. One never knows where things may lead. Opportunities with a lot of risks could falter as fast as be realized. I was part of a start-up at the very nascent signs of an open source movement. The first little start-up company was a development shop. The founder invited me to join to help invent a compelling and investment worthy product. In short, we spent long working days and nights to invent one of the first ever Linux Software driven web-serving appliances. We were just on our second round of funding when I got what turned into my from rags to riches call.

Red Hat, which was still an unknown start-up, recruited me to join that executive leadership team. It was hard won luck, but I did not realize it at the time. I just loved new technologies and working in start-ups to grow something great. We had less than twenty-five or thirty employees at the time. It's a story of its own. I was very fortunate to be part of the start-up growth story: an executive woman in technology and on the team, leading us to one of the most successful IPOs of that time. It was an incredible experience. I was fortunate, but I did my part to create that great fortune. I know this now! It took many minds around the table to create something this disruptive but not without stress, anxiety, and painful moments. This was the opportunity that led to a personal story of rags to riches— much on paper, but a happy amount in my savings. As you read earlier, growing from rags to riches is far more fun than the opposite trip.

In 2008 things took a turn for the worse for many people, and we did not escape the downturn. I watched our savings accounts slowly deplete while addicted to the daily stock reports. Our savings were disappearing, almost over-night. The painful realization that all the hard work I'd put into my career to save for my daughter's college and our retirement had simply gone up in smoke. When my husband and I weren't crying we were laughing, as the irony that we came from nothing and there back shall we go was settling somehow. Don't get me wrong, the stress and anxiety were like aliens taking over my mind, body and what spirit I had left. But what I also knew, I could not stop for a minute believing in myself. Reinvention is not easy: it can be agonizing self-reflection, rediscovery and emotional work. I knew deep down I could rebound but it was a scary and uncertain time filled with anxiety.

Knowing everyone was experiencing some level of wealth depletion made it a little less painful. Our financial advisors shared with us during a visit to hear the status of our accounts that grown men and women were balling up on the floor in the corner of his very large beautiful conference room crying. These were the men and women who came from family money and/or had successful exits making them millions of dollars and their accounts were next to empty. Some even close to or having to declare bankruptcy.

A painful time for many people, indeed. For my husband and I, well, as I said, we could only laugh and cry and laugh again. We understood working on meaningful things drove us and that it was never about the money. Neither of us was afraid to do it all over again. Whether we made money back or not was somewhat secondary. It was about finding meaning in what we were doing. We had our business and we were used to reinventing ourselves frequently. That is what we did again, and again, and again!

Maintaining a positive outlook on life is a very important part of rebounding. That does not mean we ignore the sadness and gray days. These are the days to settle into—do nothing, cry, feel what just happened was as part of healing from a traumatic set of occurrences. Loss of anything is a mourning process. What helped me most was having a soul mate, my husband, in every step with me as we together could talk, cry, regroup, and just be there for each other. We also realized how important it was not to isolate ourselves but to open up ourselves, gathering around us great collaborators, friends and team members to support our transformations.

EXERCISE 9: REBOUND STRATEGIES

1. Get that journal out! And a box of tissues, maybe some wine and candles, and a box of colored pens!

a. Write every word you are feeling! Use the pen color you chose for mad and angry words

b. Use the pen color you chose for words of sadness

c. Use the pen color you chose to reflect the hope you feel

d. Use the pen color you chose to reflect the fears that trauma is causing you.

You will write every morning when you wake up and every evening before you go to bed for two weeks after the traumatic event.

2. On week three, continue writing all of the above. After writing one page on the above items turn to a clean page and begin to write a list of ten things you love. Every morning for two weeks do this exercise even if you feel repetitive!

3. On the fourth week, add a new page answering this question: What I want is .... If your mind goes empty, just write *What do I want* till other thoughts flow into your mind.

a. This one is a meditation chant used by people like Deepak Chopra. I will often listen to his meditations on one of the streaming services as a morning routine. I find writing this question and answering the question is a worthy exercise as I begin to take steps to what is next in my life.

Perseverance

My story is of perseverance. I believed in myself and did not allow other's judgments to stop me. As a woman in technology, it was highly unusual to receive venture funding. I have a lot of stories just on the pursuit of funding alone, but I'll save those for my next book.

The two of us, pitching for funding, presenting to VCs, found it nearly impossible! I literally nearly choked our lead VC, grabbing him by his open neck, button-down, starched-white dress shirt collar, shaking him, nicely yelling, "Give us the fucking money." He was the one person I knew believed in us. He was hesitant because his funding buddies were not as open to funding nontall, nonwhite male, nonmale start-up founders. A venture deal was often, at that time, perceived as too risky for one firm. In the end, we got our funding and off we went.

I've made millions and lost millions. Plowing forward, I love to mentor others to not give up on their ideas or dreams. I have a deep desire to help more start-up founders, especially women. I've found the not great times are really where my best lessons have been discovered. Painful? Of course, but looking back on them, I can laugh now. These painful times are what make for great lessons and a hardening of your shell to not let anything stop you if you truly believe in your ideas.

Next

Do you feel dismissed? Are you feeling lost? Can you not seem to decide on anything? There are big decisions to make and they all cost money you tell yourself. You continue the mental spiral out of control. "Why do I have to figure out my next move at twenty-nine, forty, fifty, or sixty by myself?" Am I rushing it? Am I too old now? Am I trying to make it happen? Am I not hearing, seeing, or feeling the signs in front of me to just give it all up, sell everything, and move on? I need to do something anything. Work at Starbucks, make biscotti—I don't know what, but anything has to be better than feeling like nothing."

Modeling for Growth
Starts with a Growth Mind-set!

There are many models for growth, personal and professional, that work. The idea of "fake it till you make it" is a good one most of the time, but some of us undermine ourselves by confirming daily we are just *big fakes*. You ask yourself, "Is there more to life? Is there a beautiful Christmas tree village, like in the Hallmark holiday movies, of my dreams in front of me, but I am totally blind to it all?" *Is that what my dream was about?* Wondering silently is it all a pipe dream. Worse maybe you're going darker "Do I even have a freaking dream anymore, or I am destined to live other people's dreams?" People are quick to tell you what not to do. Why would you do that? Why do this? You can't afford that or this, or you need this or that. It seems everyone has the answers to other people's lives, but not their own.

What the heck is one to do? How can you trek to your *next* if there is no destination or no journey map? Where will I find the answers? All the gurus say sit quietly, the answers will come. I think that is a sucky answer. I'm not saying it's a bad answer, however! The self-help industry is over $2 billion per year. Teaching people to sit still and listen to their intuition is a bit like hoping for some magic. There is no magic without some hard work. Even sitting still and quieting your mind is hard work for many people. Finding the meaning of life is hard work. Work is hard work, and many are feeling so unfulfilled with their work that they will pay anyone to help them find a way to happiness. What are we all searching for? If giving ourselves away for free to help someone eat or build a tiny hut home to house their children makes us happy, why don't we do more giving?

Part of the solution to finding your next may just be in donating your time. Volunteering for a cause you feel strongly about can be a great way to take a break from thinking about you and your next to considering others that are in need. And by the way, a lot of very interesting people are also volunteering and getting involved so you have great potential to expand your network to people doing interesting things. Just the act alone may open your mind up to new ways of thinking.

ALL THAT I AM: NOW THAT I KNOW

CHAPTER *14.*

BREAK FROM YOUR "I DON'T KNOW-ZONE"

Break Free Steps:

1. Waste an abundant amount of time doing nothing that equates to production. Have fun going to a park and swinging or riding the merry go round. Or go for a walk. Or just sit quietly.

2. Read a few of my personal favorite books, listed below:

    a. *The Artist's Way*, by Julia Cameron
    b. *You Are a Badass*, by Jen Sincero
    c. *Declutter Your Mind*, by Steve Scott
    d. *Big Magic*, by Elizabeth Gilbert
    e. *Power of Now*, by Eckhart Tolle
    f. *21 Lessons for the 21st Century*, by Yuval Noah Harari

3. List ten values you believe in. Who are you at your core?

4. List ten new ideas each day after you finish your morning journal or anytime. Any ideas at all that come to mind that interest you are good ideas. These can be new ideas or just personal interests of yours. Write them down.

5. Create four of those ideas.

6. Pilot two of those ideas.

7. Pick one of the pilots.

Are we too deep into Oprahisms? Are we all becoming gurus of something? That would be eight billion gurus on the planet. Left to your own devices to figure out what's next, what are you a guru at?

EXERCISE 10: LIST YOUR BEST TRAITS, YOUR AWESOMENESS, AND YOUR GURUNESS!

This is no time to be modest! Write this list in your journal. Add to the list over time and reflect back on it often.

Ten thousand hours, from the book, is based on a deliberate practice to become world class in any field. Below are a few examples of possible ten thousand hours of experience:

-decision-making

-expert in communications

-visionary leadership

-problem solver

-creating new ideas

-master at connecting people

-arbitration

-music—mastery of the guitar, piano, voice, etc.

-writer

CHAPTER 15.

LIVING BOLD

Levels of Bold, Untethered, Fearlessness

I'm fortunate to have worked with a Raleigh-based organization focused on international relations. The efforts were broad, the connections wonderful. Being a female entrepreneur in a community known around the world for its research center, Research Triangle Park (RTP), was timely. The RTP area is all about fostering innovation, building start-up communities, connecting industries, university, and government research initiatives together. I achieved some successes, understood failure all too well, and gained great strength throughout my career. I participated as a mentoring member in many organizations to help start-ups achieve success. It's a passion of mine.

The US State Department formed a program many years ago to help women interested in starting micro and macro ventures in underdeveloped countries. The State Department, through its partner organizations, organized and hosted women from regions all over the world. I was fortunate enough to be invited to host our region's international women entrepreneur visitors. Thirteen to as many as twenty women at a time would join me in the sessions. Multiple simultaneous interpreters would join the women who did not speak English, interpreting our conversation in multiple languages, sharing struggles, success tips, and strategies. These women came prepared with many questions.

The visiting women's stories of enduring strength getting out of war-torn regions, battles of abuse and mistreatment, braving trips to the airport hoping bullets and bombs did not stop them made my own challenges seem petty and insignificant. Brave women traveled from Afghanistan, Pakistan, Uzbekistan, India, Egypt, Israel, Peru, and Argentina, just to name a few countries. Though worlds apart, we bonded on overcoming adversities regardless of the circumstances. Finding internal strength to rebuild after trauma, pain, and/or challenge has common strategies. Make no mistake, these women taught me more than I felt I could ever teach them. They were awe-inspiring.

5 Key Strategies to Help Overcome Challenges:

A community is always a big support system. Even when you feel there may not be one around you, find one person, then they find one person, and on until you have your own tribe. This tribe of people with common ideals and interests can be there to support you on your journey, and you can support them on theirs.

Think big, write down your vision of where you want to go then act on this vision one step at a time. I met a Latin American woman who nearly died at the beating her husband's hands. Out of desperation for her life and the safety of her children she was determined to get out. After some research, she found a small micro-loan organization that helped her buy a goat. The goat produced milk to feed her children and the children of other women in the community. They paid for the milk. She eventually bought another goat and another and then a small sack of seeds and began growing vegetables. She hid her money from her husband. His money always went to buying beer and other items that did not benefit the family. As she grew and became more self-sufficient, she started to help other women start their own businesses to do the same. She left her husband with the children and continued to grow her farm. At the time of her visit with me, she'd become the largest farm in her region. Her story was inspiring to me. I vowed to keep helping women all over the world. Big visions are great. Small steps are necessary to get there.

Seek out support systems! I never realized this program for global women existed. There are many supports, but it takes time and digging to find them. Don't stop looking. Apply to many types of funding. Do your homework. Funding or not, there are ways to take very small steps on the way to building a successful empire. It may take some patience, creativity and working three jobs while you make it happen but don't give up. If your ideas are bigger and you need larger funds, then seek out supports for how to start your business. There are many programs, start-up incubators, and organizations today helping start-ups and women with their ideas.

Stay true to who you are and your purpose. The more others offer to help listen. But you don't always have to take their advice. Take what works for you, but do listen. Acknowledge you may not know what you don't know and be open to help. You could or should do this or that. Don't veer if it does not meet your vision. Everyone means well. Their ideas may also be very good. Keep a log of these as you might come back to them later.

Dig deep inside you. There is a burning need. Some of these women had a burning need for sheer survival and their children's wellbeing. They wanted to give their children a real chance in life. Others had a burning need to change the world. All these women had real fire in their souls. They wanted to sing their messages to the world. Such passion is addictive. What is inside of you? An art brush ready to move from your mental painting to the canvas. Your breathy song on the stage of life, inspiring others to sing at the top of their lungs. Find it. Don't wait. Do it now!

CHAPTER 16.

NEW YORK, NEW YORK, NEW YORK—CRAVING FOR ENERGY

Craving for More!

It's a journey, one where sometimes you don't have an end point. You don't have a navigation system. You can't see, because the fog is incredibly dense, yet somehow you are not lost!

These journeys are the boldest of them all. They teach us the value of vision. But getting lost feeds the imagination center of our souls if we let it. The art of being lost, maybe even bored with life, with the same ole same ole, is unsettling. It's the part of life that says we may have emptied our gas tank. Empty—my head is empty, and my gut is empty with this nagging burning sensation. My heart and soul and mind are screaming, "There has to be more to life!"

I hear you loud and clear. This is a scary time. Uncertainty paralyzes us in many ways. Fear creeps in. But what if the lessons in life come from these times more than any other time. Our life—not others, not your friends, your work life, your boss's life, your mom's, or dad's, but your life. What if you choose to sit quietly with yourself for days or a month or months? What if?

I fought it, hard, for twenty-five years, never taking more than seven to ten days off every few years and typically staying connected working through vacations. I got to that point of feeling sick deep inside going to work every day doing work that felt meaningless. I fought taking time off in 2018, even though the most creative time of my life was when I did just that. Fifteen years ago I took a month off from working and took my thirteen-year-old daughter to NYC for a month. We rented an apartment and I did nothing but feed her as much dance, arts, music and theater as she could handle or wanted. During the day I simply sipped coffee and tea, and I wrote every day. I write every day now, but there is a difference in creative writing, freely digging soulfully deep and business writing no pretty fluff words, nothing really heartfelt and please no mushy or venting writing. Spending a month in NYC was only economically feasible because it was right after 9/11 and NYC begged for people to come back and not be afraid.

I've always fed on the energy of NYC. But to have the luxury of the month with my daughter in one of the most vibrant cities in the world doing nothing but sipping tea or coffee and writing while she was in classes was simply amazing. Let me be clear, it was *bold*, and I never would have done it without the nudging of a methodically put together proposal written by my daughter on why she needed to go before she was too old to be a singer or dancer.

That was nearly twenty years ago. I started my business in 2002, Creative Leadership Adventures—reinvented the business 2009 to what is now Plazabridge Group. I got clear about my business during my time in NYC. Writing every day. It actually didn't matter what I wrote. Somehow clarity emerged from the daily logs. I wanted to do more than just my business of consulting on innovation. I am creative at heart, a musician who loves writing and composing songs. Being in NYC for the summer with my daughter I realized after a certain age there are few outlets for original artists. I founded a not for profit called Night of Dreams (NOD)—a music, arts, and theatrical production organization for the benefit of raising money for charities. NOD was one of the most rewarding things I've ever done.

Night of Dreams was feeding me in ways I'd not expected, supporting the community of artists producing original productions. Creating with some of the most incredible artists in the community, many of which were involved with known bands or shows like Cirque Du Soleil, feed my creative side and also opened me up to even bigger possibilities. I wrote it out, I felt it, saw it, envisioned it all down to the voices and original music I heard in my head. What happened shocked me more than anyone could imagine! It sounds corny but it's true, these sounds in my head, the artists I dreamed of were walking in my door to audition. Bright, talented, caring, creative, giving people inspire me! They inspire me to be bold and a better version of me.

Fast forward nearly twenty years: Why the hell am I fighting to take a month off to go to Spain and hike the Camino de Santiago? This may not feel bold to you, but to me taking a month off to hike a trail and visit Spain was a *bold* notion. Biting the bullet and at the coxing— OK, strong nudging of my husband, who was going with or without me. Are you getting this picture? Some people need strong nudging, and some are the nudgers. Guess which one I am when it comes to taking time for me or time off work?

I feared taking time away from work and from our customers. I feared not having enough money for retirement or for food. I feared being homeless! These fears rise up at 3:00 a.m.—they bore deep into my being, so much so I wake in a soaking sweat. Anxiety sets in, and I feel like I want to throw up. When I am in this fear mode, I will put on my headset playing Deepak Chopra or some other mediation channel in hopes the meditation will calm me to sleep. Spending the money and not feeling like I am bringing money in the door unnerve me. My parents were very frugal! My grandparents immigrated from Lebanon, a country that has been demolished and rebuilt more times than I can count. The idea of reinventing yourself is one that comes from my heritage. The Lebanese people rebuilt their country over and over from the harshest of circumstances. I can certainly rebuild my life, my business, my family, my career. I can reinvent myself over and over again.

My grandparents fled a war-torn country split by religious conflict. I was once told that good-hearted Lebanese people will give themselves a way to help others as my ancestors did. I recently learned there is a statue honoring my great grandfather in the town my mom's family is from in Lebanon. There is something inherent in me to work hard and then work harder. Taking time off is not part of my psyche but I am learning. Taking time away from my business is like putting income on hold. This thought has a paralyzing effect on me. What happened this year when I finally called Delta and rebooked my ticket—I canceled the year before, mind you. We planned to spend the month of July hiking the Camino and exploring parts of Spain that we love and had never been to before.

A *bold* move for me, *yes*! And one of the most amazing experiences of my life. What did I learn? Why is this story important to share with you? When I ask you to write what you want, what is your answer?

What Do You Want to Do With the Rest of Your Life?

"I don't know." I hear it all the time. I've said it too many times. When asked these two little questions, people stop in their tracks. I see tears form, sweat beading on foreheads, anxiousness on faces, hands rubbing together and nervous twitches. It's such a simple question, but the answer feels life-ending.

EXERCISE 11: GET YOUR "KNOW ON"

This exercise is designed to help you become more and more clear on what you want to create in your life. It is not a one time and done exercise but one you will come back to time and time again.

Stop right now and do this exercise:

1. Get that journal out and write at the top of a page in your journal or notebook "What do I want?" List one hundred things you want in life. No rules, no barriers to your answers.

   a. Just write, start with ten things you want in your life.
   b. Then write ten things you love and want more of in your life.
   c. Write in order of importance your priorities and a sentence on each of these about how well you are doing focusing on these priorities.

Why is this exercise important? Because as you write lists, after number three, the items get harder and harder for some of us lost souls. The more we dig into "What I Want Is' the more we dig deeper inside of our psyches to get beyond what our ego wants or needs, to what really feeds our souls. What I want is to be passionate about what I do for work, I want to spend more time with my family and create stronger, more meaningful friendships! I want to be able to eat a bagel with cream cheese and not worry about gaining weight! I want to ride a horse on a big white sandy beach with my hair flowing in the wind and feel like I am thirty years old with not a care in the world! I want to be respected in the world of technology leadership for what I bring to the table.

What Do You Want?

2. Now write at the top of the page: What I want to do with the rest of my life is:

3. Write your answer in less than ten words. You cannot use these words: *but, if, maybe, might,* or *when.*

4. Repeat #3.

5. Repeat #3

Again, doing these daily exercises will only improve your ability to get what you really want in life. Your quest to the universe may be answered without even asking!

Trauma Does Not Make an Appointment

What's not to love about NYC, unless it's the absolute worst time of your life? The best and the worst time can coincide colliding into an entangled mess of emotions. Trauma hits when it wants. You cannot plan it or plan for it. There is no use in fearing it because it only cripples you for no reason. When an entangled web of events hit my life like an unplanned, explosive fireworks show in my gut and blew up everything I knew to be true I had two options: let it kill me or keep walking, albeit slowl,y into the future, one psych visit at a time.

I had just taken a role from a new company headquartered at Forty-Second Street and Third Avenue, near Grand Central Station. Let's call them "Smilecrosoft." My stays were a combination of boutique hotels or the corporate apartments on First Street near the water or the apartment on the Upper West side of New York, my personal favorite part of NYC. I was flying back and forth from Raleigh to NYC to work in New York from Monday to Thursday every week for over a year for work. It was a new job and a wonderful opportunity and a bit of a dream come true! I was to design an innovative new business division and incubate it inside the company. Going the paces was great fun—business planning, earning seed funds from inside, rapid prototyping, piloting, soft-launching, and then finally hard launching our new business. What a great experience and a wonderful opportunity. The most amazing part of this story is this opportunity was introduced to me by one of the artists in Night of Dreams. Doing good does find its way back to you.

Meetings with the company's board of directors and executive and staff team meetings took up my days, traveling to customer sites, hiring, basically never getting any alone time took up about every waking minute. Every waking minute seemed to also take up my midnight and predawn hours. In between these hours is when the tears could flow freely, the sobbing could be as loud as I uncontrollably wanted and my long healing process could take shape.

Looking back on it, the work that had to be done was not easy, it was hard work—twenty-four hours per day type of work. When in my office with the door closed, tears would well up. At night it was the work together with family. We were healing together. Long and hard work, but family is everything to me—my priority.

UNEXPECTED, UNPLANNED, SHOCK

I write with great sadness. I was sitting in a coffee shop and received a call recently from one of my former employees. I could hear it in his voice, he was about to share something awful with me, but I would have never imagined the shocking news he delivered. His business partner, also someone who previously worked for me, had committed suicide the night before. Devastating news! It rocks one's world no matter how strong you are.

I did my best to console him. I could hardly imagine the thoughts that I imagined was going through his mind. Yes, including what about the business? This was a partnership made in heaven. They'd started the business together, though they knew each other like the back of their hands. They roomed together and hiked together. They invested together and planned every aspect of their business together. They'd thought through everything. They were close friends having dinners with their girlfriends together and enjoying living a young life. Then it all appeared! But truth lurked just below the surface. The big *what-if*! What if things go terribly wrong? What if something happens to a key person in the company? What if I lose my best friend and colleague never knowing this very secret side of him or her?

As I was writing this, I realized my stories may impact more than women. Lessons may help anyone straddling the entrepreneurial cliff, teetering on success, teetering on self-confidence, teetering on extreme feelings of isolation and self-loathing. I grapple with the loss, by suicide, of a successful twenty-nine-year-old entrepreneur who was a former colleague and team member working for my company. He had everything. He had accomplished many life goals, he had traveled the world, he had a wonderful family and girlfriend, and he had the best business partner a person could have—a very close friend of mine.

Then the call no one ever wants to get—came. It took only a

nanosecond for my friend's shock, pain, horror, tears, and a lightning bolt of shock shoot straight through the phone straight into my heart. I hurt for the family. I hurt for the loss of a young life by his own choice or for any reason, but I hurt even more for his closest friend, his trusted business partner and for what they had together. The loss is very sad. The aftermath is both a mental struggle and a messy set of puzzle pieces thrown all over the place that must be pulled back together.

Now for my friend, the task at hand was to continue moving forward after a very harsh and cold stop. But how? These aren't choices we want to have to make and are rarely ever prepared for. All too often, change is forced upon us for reasons we just can't fathom. My friend's initial reaction was: "I'll have to close the business." His partner ran the back-end operations and the finances, and my friend ran front end, sales, marketing, and customer relations. In the heat of the moment, the feeling was there was no way he could continue building this successful business without his partner and friend.

Life is filled with twists and turns. When we least expect it, the universe tosses a most unexpected challenge. My own life has been disrupted at varied times by financial loss, challenges in my marriage, and the loss of beloved family members. There is no planned timing for these. There is no set-aside budget to deal with the repercussions of these events; they just happen and knock us off our rocker! Maybe yours is the loss of the largest customer you've had for years changing course and pulling their multimillion-dollar account from you. In any event, these surprises feel like an explosive disruption to life as we knew it.

It happened to me, to my friends, and to my colleagues. No one is immune. Simple actions like putting one foot in front of the other are nearly impossible. Our minds turn on us, and we look for reasons why this all happened.

Transformation often is an outcome of traumatic events. For me it was certainly the case. I can only speak to my own events and those who were brave enough to share experiences they went through. For me the transformation took me to a new level of awareness of my own emotions. I'll share some strategies that I used to heal and kick my journey back on the path I deeply wanted to travel.

It is important to understand that posttraumatic growth is more than mere resilience in the face of trauma. The big difference is change. Resilience is when you get punched, stagger and then jump right back up.

Posttraumatic growth is different: When you stand back up, you are transformed."

Survivors build new lives around the traumatic event, and they move on—they build a new life outside of their pain.

—Lawrence Calhoun

A traumatic event—whether a sudden loss of a job, a start-up failure, the loss of a loved one, or a betrayal by a friend—are all sobering events that disrupt our lives. You may experience a number of traumatic events in your lifetime. Resiliency is a necessary part of life! Be kind to yourself after a traumatic event. I will cry; I will hurt! Hurt a lot! I feel the anger and give myself permission to feel all the emotions. But resilience taking the steps forward and resolving or forgiving the past so I can move forward. Reflection is a big part of reinvention and rebounding. I will reflect but then know I must get back up, dust myself off, and keep walking.

Transformation from a traumatic event may incentivize the need for life changes. No, this is not easy. It was not for me and or any people I've worked with, however, life will continue and you can make it through. Maybe using a few of these strategies will help.

EXERCISE 12: DRAMA RECOVERY

I have experienced holding in, not talking about my traumatic experiences, keeping it all in and to myself—to the point of nearly breaking down. Holding on to trauma and not sharing your emotions can eat away at your insides, eat at your mental power and leave you with a feeling of helplessness. But there is a way out, a way toward being stronger than you were before. A new normal, a better you, and a stronger you for sure.

Charting your own path to opening up will be important and possibly necessary to keep your sanity and allow you to reach that growth-full new normal state! Write, writ, write. Write angry letters to someone you are mad at or that hurt you. But throw them away! It serves no purpose to send them to anyone. Writing angry letters is only to clear your mind of angry, ugly thoughts! Get them out of your being so you can be a new you!

Then:

1. Talk! Talk to therapists if you cannot talk to anyone else. If you can seek out friends, mentors or people who you feel will be there for you, talk. Talking it out is part of the healing process.

2. Feel the pain until it subsides. This is the hardest part because it feels sucky. You may think you are losing your mind; you may think that people think you are losing your mind. It doesn't matter what they think. Write out how you feel. Writing your anger and sadness out on paper is another form of talking. This is not a journal to be shared. You may choose to tear up every page and toss them, but release this pain in some form to the universe.

3. Search deep inside for those things that bring you joy and do some of those things. Is it music? It is art? Is it a new hobby? Yoga, meditation, walking in the woods are all wonderful soulful inside search activities.

4. Give yourself permission not to rush the healing process. For me it took over a year until I felt some semblance of feeling a new normal.

5. Traumas tend to have tentacles connecting us to other past traumas. If you've been through a trauma and have not worked yourself through that trauma emotionally and then go through another life-altering event, the trauma may feel connected. Don't discount your past. Tying these feelings together will only allow for a greater transformative experience if you work through the emotions. Working through the emotional effects may need more help than just these exercises. Seek outside help if needed.

6. Reinventing oneself is a constant demand in life. Recognize, when you are ready to find a brighter light, this is another opportunity to grow in ways you did not realize that it was ever possible. I promise this is a bright silver lining behind those dark clouds.

Transformations can help shed fears from our psyches. We may form new fears but shedding old fears allows for growth in new ways. Explore what you no longer fear! Fear is our friend at times, as it raises the hairs on the back of our necks when something just does not feel right. If you have a queasy feeling in your stomach because you want to get on stage and sing to the top of your lungs because your life dream is to sing in front of a live audience, do it now! If you feared parachuting before the shit fall of traumatic events changed your life forever do it now! But realize lasting change is inherent in you now and stepping out of bounds to start a new venture, a new relationship, an endeavor is always inside of you. Take baby steps toward these new adventures on your personal journey. Think big, dream big, but take the small steps to get you there.

CHAPTER 17.

FALLING, FEARING, FAILING, FROLICKING

Forward Rolling

What is it about the word *fail* that we fear to the point of paralyzing our every movement? People fear the craziest things. From getting on an escalator to flying across the ocean to starting a business or to speaking our thoughts and truths in meetings. Paralyzed movements hold us back from achieving some of life's greatest gifts. Maybe we don't date a guy for fear thinking he'll end up not liking us. Maybe we don't start our own business for fear of failing and going broke. Maybe we don't go skiing for fear of falling down. How might we learn new things if we fear doing them? What are we really fearful of?

One of my greatest fears is forgetting the words to songs when I am singing for events or speaking at an engagement. I once knew a chief marketing officer of one of the largest Fortune 100 companies around the globe who had panic attacks when just thinking about speaking in public. A founder of a very successful growth company feared losing everything and not having enough for retirement. The fear held her back from making critical decisions on where to invest in the business. This stalled growth and in turn started to turn the company on a downward spiral. The competition began stealing their customers, and they were not able to keep up with the competition.

First of all, there's no denying these are real feelings. The emotions of fear are not to be ignored. However, we can manage our way through them to the other end of achieving the very thing we feared most. No, it's not always easy, but with some simple steps, we can manage our way through the fear.

How did I manage my fear of forgetting my words to songs or speeches? Yes, I agree, this may sound like a simple fear, but it kept me from performing on bigger stages and bigger events much of my life. I finally faced my fear in a few steps. The first one was to gain more experience performing with groups and with other people. I enrolled in a 'Women that Rock' weekend music retreat. The goal of this retreat for me was to improve my performance skills, my guitar playing and to break down my fear of forgetting my words. By the way, you do not have to already be a musician to join a program like this! A wonderful event this was for sure. I met some amazing women, and incredible musicians. We wrote new songs together, worked on songs I had written, and practiced our performing. The most profound thing happened on the very first day. As we went around in a circle, sharing what we wanted to get out of the program, I shared my fear, as did everyone else. From that day on, we helped everyone get over their fears. The instructor's first statement to me was to stop being afraid of forgetting my words, we'll just write them all out on cue cards. You can read them while performing.

I know, *right*? This simple strategy I'd thought of before but did not ever give myself permission to do, because I thought it would make me appear weak, silly, and not a real musician. Little did I know, many of the world's best musicians use these strategies. For example, most use earpieces with words being recited to them. Now I actually market myself as a glasses-wearing, music-stand-bearing musician whose passion is musical performances; and my glasses-wearing, music-stand-bearing band does too. It's how we market ourselves; it's our theme!

EXERCISE 13: BATTLING FEARS

Tactics to Help You Battle Fears:

1. Find yourself a fear buddy. A friend or colleague who you can share your deepest fears with. You share yours, and he or she will share theirs with you.

    a. It's important to write these down and monitor triggers. A trigger is something that may set off the rallying cry in the pit of your stomach, building up to a cold sweat and possibly even an anxiety attack in some people. These are real feelings, but they may not be presenting a real life-threatening danger. Triggers, like intuitions, are there to protect you from real danger. The job at hand with your fear buddy is to help identify what is real and what are imagined worries that are causing you to *stop* in your tracks, paralyzed.

    b. Write down these triggers as soon as you feel them coming on. Also, write down when you have a clear mind and can identify what may have caused the buildup of fear.

    c. Not all fears cause stress or anxiety. Some fears are blockers, blocking you from making a decision or moving forward on something. When you feel you have a wall or barrier in front of you and you just can't seem to move forward. These may be potential fears keeping you from your best self or your company's growing success. What do you look forward to but it makes you nervous? Can you identify the blockage you feel in doing that thing?

    i. You point to everyone else as the cause of something not happening

    ii. You fire good people for no reason

    iii. You wake up at 3:00 a.m. in a cold sweat after a nightmare of your office burning down

    iv. You wake up at 3:00 a.m. and start immediately firing off emails

    v. You wake up at 2:00 a.m. and start building a to-do list two miles long in your head only to have forgotten every item on the list by 8:00 a.m. in the office.

    vi. Write your own here_____

2. Join a group that would allow you to safely face your fear. Joining a music performance group allowed me a safe environment to work out my fears with new strategies. This effort tapped into my creative side and opened me up to other possibilities.

3. Tiptoe your way into the fear. If you fear to ride death-defying roller coasters—start with the baby coaster and work your way up. Don't parachute from twenty thousand feet without first bungee jumping one thousand feet.

4. Reentry: Leave the confines of your head and enter the scary space of the outside world.

Finding your buddy may be challenging, but my suggestion is to start with someone you can trust deeply to be honest with you. A buddy may be a very trusted advisor who you know you can count on, telling you the truth and helping to breakdown fears into manageable chunks of action. It could be a very close friend who has common goals, and you know you can count on them to step in when needed. In one example, I have two such friends. If we text 911 support to each other we know to pick up the phone and call. That 911 support text or call is our way of saying I need to talk this out and get someone with a level head to talk me off a cliff. Help me through a situation. I know these few close friends will be there for me.

CHAPTER 18.

PLEASE SAY YES! HOW TO INFLUENCE DECISION MAKERS

There is an art to getting what you want, deserve and need for work and life. The art of influence is a subtle practice in negotiations that do not feel like negotiations—a practice of being believable, credible information and having the support of others around you who will support your ideas. Whether your need is for a raise in your salary, a need to relocate to a new region of the country, or if it's an idea you feel would be the next world-changing idea, there is work to be done to convince others to work with you.

Asking for relocation in a company can be daunting. For me, I knew I had to leave Houston but did not want to leave my company at the time. Houston served me well, but it no longer fit my want list. It was too hot, too humid, and too far from my family.

I understood that *simply* asking to be moved to a new region may not yield the result I hoped for. I was the number one salesperson in a region during a time when the rest of the company was experiencing a bit of a downtrend in sales. My sales were exploding. Should I move? If I were to move, it would possibly cause my boss not to earn his bonus for hitting his numbers. What needed to be done? I needed to build a case for my move and ensure the right people, those who could make a financial decision on supporting a move and allow me time to relocate, understood the benefits of me relocating. In other words, what's in it for them? Not just the company but each coworker supporting me on this move. I needed to share what they get out of me moving. How will they benefit? Let me build a landscape of how this process would work.

First there is my boss. If I move, he potentially loses his bonus as the cost of my move would be out of his budget. He possibly may not be able to replace me or it may take months and he will have to do more with less.

Next there is the new regional director. If I transfer to a new region, they have to absorb my quota into their numbers, which would increase their goals by more than $6 million dollars and increase the risk of not hitting his or her numbers, thus no bonus for them.

Then there is the cost of relocation. The cost of the relocation, $20,000, would have to come out of one of the regional director's budget.

And then there is the company overall. As a public company, there is the risk of missing a quarter's revenue goals. If I miss my numbers by being distracted with a move it could impact the company overall.

Are you getting this picture? This is not about what I want solely. My needs and desires have great impacts on others if not fully thought through. How do I make my case and get to the decision I want? I need to also frame it so it proves positive for everyone. Here is how I managed to get my ASK!

First, I needed the information. I did research on what region's had strong potential growth regions. Could I possibly even double the region's sales numbers? I reviewed opportunities around the country. Where were these opportunities not being realized? Second, I studied the boundaries of the regions and the directors of those regions. Were there any gray areas? For example, was there a region that reported to a manager that had a gap in the sales team? Third, I identify trends in the world that may help my case. Fourth, I needed to build a case—a justification for my move.

    a. What could I prepare that answered all the possible concerns that would come up?

    b. How quickly could I show a return on the investment for my move? In other words, how quickly could I grow revenue in the new region?

    c. What could I do to show how my boss and his boss and the company would benefit from approving my relocation?

Here Is How It All Came to Pass

My justification included a very strong WSJ article sharing how difficult it was to find top sales talent around the world and companies should invest in keeping their top talent happy, feeling motivated and show them future opportunities for themselves. Then I proposed that my move to Northern Virginia would be a great location. No one was mining nonfederal business. I proposed that I start up the commercial division in the market working out of the federal office covering five states. I proposed that I could report under my current boss since the region was new—he gets his bonus!.

And I proposed a transition plan for my old region ensuring the new region director would have a successful start.

Win, Win, Win, and Sold!

EXERCISE 14: KEY STRATEGIES YOU CAN USE:

1. Research: Who is affected, how will it impact any stakeholders, what is in it for them and the company. Or if this is a personal quest, who is impacted and what motivates them, what's in it for them.

2. Identify all the people who can a) support you, b) be affected by any decisions made and c) may not see any reason to support you. Understand their point of view (POV).

3. Build your case: Writing this case out will help you articulate and talk it out. If you have a personal goal and you need people and funds, craft a strong story that emotionally connects with those you want to help you. What's in it for them? Why would they want to help you or invest in your venture? Practice answering this question with friends and close colleagues you trust. Get their feedback then adjust your message.

CHAPTER 19.

THE FOX, THE BEAR AND THE BLACK WIDOW

In many companies, in friend circles, cliques, at school, in charities and nonprofits, even working with volunteers, wherever you are, there are foxes, bears, and black widows lurking.

If you are the founder and have employees working for you, observe the small groups that form. Get to know what motivates and drives your staff. Motivations may mostly be healthy for your company and for the people in the company.

144

However, other motivations may bite you or take you by surprise, leaving you floundering and asking yourself, *What just happened?*

First, the fox: Foxes are a quiet, brilliant animal. Foxes prefer to remain inconspicuous. They choose subtlety and cunningness over brute strength. They may be quiet contributors, only speaking to those with influence and listening quite attentively. The fox may give credit where credit is due. As a leader of your organization, ask the fox how these ideas came to pass. The fox may share all insights as it helps to validate their feedback, insights, and ideas.

The bear is a very social animal with surprising intelligence. Bears often share friendship, resources, and security. They form hierarchies and have structured kinship relationships. Bears can be fierce competitors when feeling threatened or when their cubs are close by. Help bears feel wanted, needed and valued. Recognize them and their cubs for their contributions.

Then there is the black widow, whose bite may not be felt immediately. They lurk quietly building a web of protection around them and when a moment presents itself, they strike. A black widow has the potential to be the most disruptive person in your organization. Their intentions are not always honorable. You may never see the web they build around them. Maybe your intuition has the hair standing straight up on the back of your neck, but you can't put a finger on why. Worse, you see a trail of signs, but you discount these signs thinking it's just their personality or your intuition is off. Everything will work out for the best. Maybe you do not realize that you, the *founder of your* company, are the target of the black widow's strike. For example, an investor suggests a key talent take over the business development function in your newly funded organization. You agree and place them in only to be replaced by this individual six months later. Feeling like you were hit by a bus, you ask yourself repeatedly how did this happen? What could I have done? What signs are you seeing or feeling? Keep a log of your observations.

All this to say people are complicated, and start-ups can be stressful. Building a strong people culture and really protecting that culture is one of the most important things a founder can do. Allow your team members to provide quarterly feedback. Have an open-door policy to express concerns and address these concerns in the moment. Don't take one person's word as truth without checking in with others. People are challenging, but open communications, frequent check-ins, employee engagement activities and a strong feedback system will help you identify any early warning signs or risks.

CHAPTER 20.

NEEDING LESS-GAINING MORE

Less is far harder than more. You may not believe me. Let's try an exercise. Sit in a comfortable place in your home or apartment and take a long inventory look at your surroundings. Books, pictures, knick-knacks on shelves, furniture, collectibles, rugs, pictures on the wall, TV, stereo— take it all in. Now do the same for each room. If you only have two rooms, do it for those two rooms. If you have sixty rooms do this exercise for all sixty rooms. Mentally inventory everything you have in your living quarters.

Now for the exercise: the only thing you own now is a large hiking backpack. What would you take from home that can fits in your backpack? Consider this is all that you can carry on your back, and you are leaving everything else behind to charity or selling it. What do you take? What do you *need*? Need is the operative word here. It's what you need to keep you warm, dry, fed, protected, shoed, and clean—nothing else, really.

Now that you have this list of items, how do you declutter and rid your life of all that is unnecessary? This may feel drastic but it's an important exercise even if it's only a mental exercise. Downsizing can be an emotional set of events. I know, as my husband and I have walked away no less than two times from all that we owned. The first time was when moving from Houston and relocating to Northern Virginia. As you read above, I lobbied my move and was appointed the new territory. Then the second, more recent downsizing, selling our home of twenty-plus years, selling and giving away as much as we could, including twenty years of collected furniture, books, and glasses. Over two hundred wine and drinking glasses were given away, and I don't even know how we collected this many over that time.

The first resizing of our life took place when I was in my midthirties. It was by accident not conscientiousness. We wanted to create a more sustainably responsible life, so my husband and I just decided to walk away from all that we

148

owned in our thirty-three-hundred-square-foot home. We gave away or sold everything except my little four-year-old daughter's belongings and furniture. We packed up dishes, sold couches, sold our newly purchased large comfy chairs. We sold wall hangings, bedroom furniture, and office furniture. All that we had was either sold or given away, including a treasured upright piano.

We wanted to start fresh, reinvent ourselves, and create a cleaner, freer way of living. Our move into a very small two-bedroom apartment was our holding tank for a transformative life. It was one of the happiest times ever. It felt worry free. We needed nothing but the essentials, mattress on the floor, bean bag chair in the living room and a few small things we added slowly over time. Slowly we added valuable pieces like getting incredibly lucky to buy a beautiful baby grand piano. A husband of a divorcing couple wanted to rid of his home of the gift he bought his soon to be ex-wife. Ouch for him but yay for us. It was a steal! I cherish this piano to this day Of course, it will not fit in my backpack. The effort of leaving stuff behind and starting over is a mentally cleansing event. It can be difficult to declutter one's life. It takes time, and if you are married or have a significant other, it helps to have you both be of a mind to declutter at the same time.

The second such downsizing event was just a few years ago. Our daughter was in her twenties and starting on her way to shaping her world surroundings. We'd been unsuccessfully trying to sell our home for a few years. Our downsizing efforts had been going on over those years, holding yard sales, making donations, and giving stuff away. Every spring and fall we found there were new boxes of stuff, more that could go, stuff in closets and drawers forgotten about for years. I felt after many of these yard sales and giveaways that we'd be down to the bones ridding ourselves of stuff. Then one day, frustrated that we could not sell our home for the price we wanted I created an Airbnb profile to just test the waters on renting our home out.

I'd only started the Airbnb profile, adding a few pics and listing the location, thinking I would come back and finish it later that evening. I made my initial profile public and to my surprise had more than four requests in the first fifteen minutes of it going live. Now really readying the home for renters was going to force us to rid our home of as much as possible. We set out to separate our belongings. Storing in a locked garage went those sentimentally treasured and valuable items and giving away even more stuff to declutter the home. This effort was far more difficult and emotional than ever imagined. It is a cleansing like no other.

Memories never leave you, but the stuff triggering memories may one day be in consideration for giving away. How could we rid our lives of stuff? This took a lot of time and a lot of tears, a lot of talking and memory sharing and maybe a bit of mourning for that life of stuff we are leaving behind. Each time the emotions weighed heavy, but the outcome post-downsize was wonderfully freeing. The more stuff owned the more emotions you may feel and the longer it may take to rid your life of these things. A friend of ours going through a similar exercise shared with us his inability to sell a full, beautiful, expensive dining-room set.

No one wanted to buy. No charity even wanted to take the furniture because of its size. He ended up posting on boards: "Free dining-room set" and finally gave it away. Memories around the table create a false value to the dining-room set itself, but the memories don't need the physical stuff. Memories are in our mind. We can create the vision of the family and friends around the table and feel those moments without the table and chairs.

What could you do today to rid yourself, and feel a little freer, of stuff? Here are some tips that I hope to make your process a little easier.

EXERCISE 15: STRATEGIES TO FEEL FREER:

1. Go through a periodic exercise, even if only a mental exercise, of the items you must have with you should

you only have a tiny house, or a backpack on your back.

2. Separate items with some form of tagging or marking you cannot see, like a small sticker underneath a couch. Remember this thing can go when the time comes. When it does come, you will be reminded of those items you know are just stuff and no longer needed

Lost in Hype

Let's also take a different look at our lives.

3. "You are as great as the top five people around you" —I hate this statement. It seems our future success depends on how successful, or not so successful, our closest five friends are. The simple truth is you may grow apart from friends. The people closest to you cannot cause you to be unsuccessful or successful. However, your growth, your goals, and passions may no longer align with those top five people around you.

   a. Take time to inventory your life. Who are your closest friends?

152

i. What advisors, employees, and colleagues do you have around you?
ii. What's missing from your close relationships?
iii. Take some steps to broaden this network.
iv. Diversify your relationships as new thinking may help you grow.

CHAPTER 21.

REAWAKENING

Cloudy with a chance of emotional storms

Emerging from a dense fog

The lightning strikes and the flowers sleep

It's time to dance

Music drenches my life

Fear is this survivor thriver's food

Done with the past

It's a reawakening of my soul

CHAPTER 22.

AND NOW THAT I KNOW

Support networks—friends—are the lifeline. Make or keep friends close to you.

Time to write the next scene in my life's journey! Write, write and write some more.

Beating the meetup syndrome! Stop fearing and start living life on your terms.

Rules? Really?

My beautiful mosaic of life—paint it! Your canvas is white and ready for your next. Visualize it on the canvas.

And my story is just beginning

Lessons for the Brave at Heart

Lead with heart, soul, and passion—there are no other options. Really, think about it. Being miserable or stressed in this journey toward entrepreneurial success is challenging enough! Why not *love* what you are doing, creating, giving, or inventing? Take some time now and rewrite your success playbook. Do so each time your heart and your head tell you it's time. This is another journaling exercise. If you aren't quite getting that the journals you are writing are your keys to your future, then hear me now: Just about every successful person says that writing is a strategic part of finding your way to big dreams, goals and designing life. Color fuels creativity. Paint your walls, your pages, your books, your clothes! Feel the freedom to create. No one will see this if you don't show it to them. It's just for you. I guarantee you if you write, color, craft, and create, over time, you will free new personal passions. Writing free-flow can be a freeing of the ideas rattling in the caves of your brain.

Live life to help others keep going. Wealth is not in the money but in the journey, in the experiences and lessons we learn and what we share to give back along our path. My motivation is to create a community for change! I use mind-shifting strategies—like learning new things—which is fuel for me. Having a growth mind-set allows me expanded thinking power.

EXERCISE 15: STRATEGIES TO INNOVATIVE IDEAS INTO ACTION!

Passion often comes from the discovery of something you would love to change. For example, a time constrained individual does not care about getting to a grocery store, walking through isles and isles of stuff and putting only what's needed into a grocery cart—frustrating! *Who has time for grocery shopping*? An online store is created for ease of shopping. New shipping methods are invented to ship right to the door—you get the picture.

Shop online! Use the time you save shopping to write a new vision for your life.

Questions to Get Your Brain Churning:

- What are you the most frustrated with either in your current business or just in life generally?

- What motivates you most? Helping people, building community, starting a community garden? Inventing technology solutions? Solutions that support the elderly or disabled?

- Where does your community need the most help?

- Are you interested in solving global issues like: water shortages, equality for women and minorities, global warming, ridding the world of plastic?

1. Consider a problem that has one of these compelling drivers:

    a. You are angry about something that never seems to work.

    b. You read about a world or community problem and wonder why someone hasn't done something about this yet.

    c. You have a passion for a particular area—say animals, children, elderly people—and want to find things that help them.

2. Pick one area that you are feeling drawn to for example: Asia is facing an age battle in the workplace. Employees thirty-five and older are no longer valued in the tech workplace. The United States has been doing this for years, but a low unemployment rate is creating opportunities for older workers. Why aren't we innovating new ways to engage all ages? Starting businesses and working at any age keeps everyone engaged in life: Working till we want to drop, giving, using our talents, art forms, skills to influence better lives. These are just a few considerations that may spark ideas of your own.

    a. Read everything you can about the challenges of aging out of the workplace.

    b. Understand the effects:

        i. Economics of aging are expensive

        ii. Loneliness is becoming an epidemic not just in aging but with everyone all over the world, particularly in the U.S.

        iii. Research – areas where countries or companies are working on solutions to see what you can learn.

3. And now the journal:

    a. Write ten to twenty ideas every day for ten days.

    b. On the eleventh day, narrow these ideas down to your top three picks.

    c. Then answer the questions below:

        i. Would you invent something new? Is that your passionate idea? There is the ability to always start a business that could be profitable. To increase the odds of success yearly planning and strategizing are important.

        ii. Would you prefer to volunteer for an organization and invent solutions together?

        iii. How might you find ways to do both!

4. Write three goals you want to achieve over the next three months to turn your ideas into action:

    a. Who can help you?

    b. What experts can you research further and who can you talk to in order to learn more.

What nonprofit organizations or for-profit companies exist that you could learn from and possibly talk to. To me, competition fuels inventiveness. Use what you learn to determine what you can do differently.

CHAPTER 23.

SERENDIPITY

Sitting by my fireplace in my new living room overlooking the mountain range, I reflect on how in the world I landed on this mountaintop. A fire sky sunset falls behind the jagged peaks. I am sipping on a pinot noir, staring out at a mountain facing our wall of windows and reflecting on how I got here. In this moment, I am overwhelmed and grateful for the journey that has landed me in the home of my dreams, albeit small, quaint, simple, but lovely).

Years ago I wrote in my journal about the view I wanted

in my life. I wanted a home and a setting that would inspire me every morning and evening. I wrote specifics. I wanted it in the mountains. I wanted my home on the top of a mountain. I describe the view from my windows and how sunrises and sunsets would look from my imaginary windows. In many of my journal entries many years ago, I painted the picture of what I wanted. Now I am sitting in our new home and have realized, to the details of my writings, a new home in the mountains.

I can laugh at the tears shed now. All those painful muscle aches from moving four times in and out of apartments and storage units as my husband and I searched for our "what's next." The 3:00 a.m. anxiety wake-up calls and the urgent need to make mental to-do lists, only to be forgotten by 8:00 a.m. I have worked hard to calm my monkey mind with hot yoga, hikes, wasting time, working the exercises in this book, and holding on to an undying belief that everything happens for a reason.

I have lived out of three storage units, moving to various cities trying to find a landing spot and define my next move. I have reinvented myself and my business so many times I lose track. Reinvention is necessary to keep pace with the artificially intelligent and exponential pace of global change. My husband and I have been through some kind of hell and back. But we never lost sight of the humor in it all. We are two people who came from modest upbringings. Not living a material life, to living a material life, to letting it all go and who needs it. We are not full-fledged minimalists but we can be and we are OK with that!

In less than three years, I have experienced every emotion you can possibly imagine. When we thought we were in heaven there was a sudden hell to overcome. But when it was all said and done, after falling down a flight of stairs and days later slipping in a garage, falling flat on my face, I stand strong and now laugh at the painful news after moving a fourth time. Feeling fortunate at the offer of friends unable to sell their home. Moving into our friend's beautiful seven-thousand-square-foot mountain, as they did not want it to sit empty, only to get the news two days after all the boxes were unpacked they'd accepted an unexpected offer on their home. We had less than three weeks to find another place to live and move out. And yes, it was during the most hectic time for my business ever, and it was the holidays! Tears flowed, poured, flowed again, and then laughter, more tears, laughter—and yes, a bit of anger, hurt, more tears, and laughter.

Searching Airbnb for something to rent in the same mountain town region, I found a quaint little seven-hundred-square-foot efficiency apartment at a tiny little mountain inn. Everything we could get back in storage went to storage. The only personal items we kept with us were the clothes we needed for work and leisure. Things were hanging from the curtain rods and piled in every little corner, but we were comfortable, warm, and actually found we enjoyed it much more than the seven-thousand-square-foot home. A hotplate and microwave replaced the beautiful chef's oven and healthy choice frozen dinners and soups replaced baked chicken and grilled ahi tuna steaks. And then, when least expected, the house of our dreams appears before us! I look back at the last four or five years and it really was all a set up to bring us here. Not without pain and emotional ups and downs, a great deal of humility and a bucket of tears.

If we'd not taken the risk to move to the big house, we may never have found the little house of our dreams. If we'd not sold our home of twenty years and paid off the debt, we may never have taken the opportunity to find our beautiful spot in the mountains. If we'd not given ourselves permission to waste time for a pilgrimage trip to Spain, we may not have had a clear mind to see a brighter future. Walking the Camino de Santiago was a gift—a gift I gave myself; a gift of learning patience. The hike proved all I need is what I can carry on my back. And most of all, the journey on foot allowed me space to quiet my monkey mind while opening space for much more to enter into my life. What's next? I don't know but I will quietly reflect, continue to write, dream, hike, reflect, learn—and yes, constantly reinvent myself and my business!

When I least expected it, the unexpected hit me square in the face, both bad and good. Being open allowed me great insight that nothing is ever as bad as it seems. It's all part of life's journey!

EXERCISE 16: PLAN YOUR OWN PILGRIMAGE

You don't have to go to Spain to hike, and you don't have to hike for days. You can hike in your own backyard. Hike for twenty minutes or one hour or all day with a picnic lunch.

1. Add a walk or hike to your week—or day—when you can. If you are finding yourself too busy at the office begin to ask for walking meetings. Getting outdoors for one on one walks or small team discussions can be an effective use of time and get you out of the office for some fresh air.

2. Plan a solitude hike, where you are alone and walking in nature for at least twenty minutes, quietly, with no headphones or music. We are a society in many ways numbing ourselves with noise. Let your mind wander in the quiet. It may be very difficult at first but the more you do this the more you will realize benefits from the quieting of your mind.

3. After each hike or walk, spend ten minutes writing in your journal. Don't think too hard about what you are writing, just write anything. Let your mind wander on the paper.

EXERCISE 17: REFLECTIONS

Self-reflection can make you a better leader and a more grounded mother, wife, partner, or individual. What might you reflect on? Your journal writings may hold hints.

1. Focus some attention on what you've have learned about yourself over the past two weeks. How have you reacted in meetings to decisions being made or request for budget funds for a new project?

2. How have you treated your staff members or better yet how have you responded to a pouting child or a request from a spouse or friend?

3. What triggers have affected you emotionally? Can you put your finger on these triggers and identify where emotional anxiety or stress may be coming from?

4. What areas of yourself do you want to develop? Do you want to take a finance class or take violin lessons? How might you round out your analytical skills with creative thinking or vice versa?

5. Reflect on the business you want? What culture do you want to create? What kind of customers/clients do you want to serve? How will you feel every day working? What would excite you about this business?

6. One of the best exercises I have used for reflecting is writing as though you have accomplished the very thing you are visioning or writing about. You are telling your grandchildren about what you created. What did you accomplish, who did it impact? How did your journey feel? Write in great detail about where you are in that future story and how you successfully created your vision.

Self-reflection is not spending hours contemplating your navel," Kraemer says. "No! It's: What are my values, and what am I going to do about it? This is not some intellectual exercise. It's all about self-improvement, being self-aware, knowing myself, and getting better.

—Harry M. Kraemer, Kellogg School of Management, Northwestern University

BONUS EXERCISE 18: CELEBRATE YOU!

It's time to take time for you and celebrate all that you have accomplished. Planning *all-about-you dates* is important. Treating yourself to little breaks or something special is a great way to celebrate you. I don't mean just going out and buying a new pair of shoes or going to a mani-pedi—these are fun, but what about taking every Friday off for the next four weeks. Use hiking, writing, yoga weekend retreats, or your favorite activity as your fuel. Give yourself the gift of days to celebrate you. These breaks may be the best thing in the world, allowing you to recharge your battery and see the world in a whole different light.

SPECIAL THANKS!

I am not sure this book would have been born without my good friend Shawn Ramsey. Thank you for all your encouragement, feedback and for the magic crystals and wonderful inspiration. Also thank you Brian Ference for your support and feedback.

ABOUT THE AUTHOR

Teresa Spangler

Serial Entrepreneur, Innovator, Advisor, Disruptor, Passionate Speaker, Author, & Lead Singer Rhythm Guitarist for the band The Headless Chickens.

Teresa Spangler has been a driving force behind innovation and growth. Today, she wears multiple hats as a social entrepreneur, innovation expert, growth strategist, author and speaker—not to mention mother, wife, bandleader, and much more. She is especially passionate about helping CEOs and entrepreneurs understand how best to navigate growth, how to value the role human

capital plays in innovation, and how to understand the impact that innovation has on humanity in our ever-increasing cyber world. Teresa shares her insights on these and more topics as a member of the Forbes Technology Council. She is the mastermind behind the GameDay Decisions Analytics Platform™, an integrated artificial intelligence and machine-learning platform as a service to "simplify the art and science of decision-making."

Teresa held executive positions at Red Hat Software, where she was responsible for leading revenue growth pre- and post-IPO. In addition, she has founded and led many entrepreneurial organizations through growth milestones including venture capital funding, IPOs, innovation consultancy, and technical services. She also founded a philanthropic performing arts organization, which created showcase opportunities for more than two hundred original artists and musicians over seven years that captured the attention of New York dance communities and globally known musicians. Teresa's passion for the arts and music can be witnessed firsthand when she performs as a singer and songwriter, guitarist, and lead singer of the Headless Chickens.

Twitter: @composerspang
LinkedIn: linkedin.com/in/teresawspangler

TERESA SPANGLER

Made in the USA
Las Vegas, NV
17 December 2021

38344213R00098